Gordon Lang
The Carnoustie Effect

CW00406387

The right of Gordon Lang to be identified as the author of this work has been asserted by him in accordance with the Copyright, Designs and Patents Act 1988

Gordon Lang
The Carnoustie Effect
Warfare in the twenty-first century
© 2002 by Verlag Siegfried Bublies, D-56290 Schnellbach, Germany
e-Mail: Siegfried.Bublies@t-online.de
All rights reserved
Printed in Germany 2002 by druck+text GmbH, Beltheim
ISBN 3-926584-76-9

Gordon Lang

The Carnoustie Effect

Warfare in the 21st century

Verlag Siegfried Bublies

By the same author in German and available from Verlag Siegfried Bublies:

"...die Polen verprügeln...", vols. I & II
Das perestrojanische Pferd

CARNOUSTIE: Golf links and small town on east coast of Scotland. Site of battle against Vikings, 1010 AD. Venue of controversial Open Golf Championship 1999, when townspeople's everyday course condemned by world's best players as 'too tough'.

CARNOUSTIE EFFECT: That degree of mental and psychic shock experienced on collision with reality by those whose expectations are founded on false assumptions.

CONTENTS   Page

THE CARNOUSTIE EFFECT

No one could blame the young men for their over-confidence.

Everywhere they had played, trophies had been theirs for the collecting. Acclamation had been accepted as their due, riches achieved by some equal to a lifetime's earnings for many of their admirers.

The young men were masters of their *métier*. They had nothing to fear.

Then they came to Carnoustie.

They found that they had spent their whole lives playing another kind of game altogether. They did not know that what was played at Carnoustie was the real, the original game of golf, that almost all other courses outside Scotland were imitations, and sanitized imitations at that.

The golf which the young men had learned was played on broad fairways, with shallow bunkers, soft ground which stopped the ball rolling away, and only a slightly less closely cropped lawn instead of genuine rough. No one had told them that this was not the real game of golf at all, that it was more like an exhibition than a struggle. They had no idea that the difference between their smoothed-down game and the real thing was the difference between flat racing and steeplechasing.

It was not the young men's fault. They had been raised with false expectations.

What they were now experiencing was the Carnoustie effect – the shock of being confronted abruptly with a reality overturning all presuppositions.

Over that same piece of North Sea coastal land, now the scene of sporting frustrations, Scots and Vikings had once fought out a battle which lasted for three days – an unusually protracted struggle in an age when issues were customarily decided on the first day of encounter. Like those unsuspecting golfers who were to follow, the invading Vikings too were thwarted – but these great warriors did not suffer the true Carnoustie effect, which can be undergone only by those who have been deluded about the task confronting them.

In that invasion year of 1010, few went into battle with unrealistic expectations. There were no supposed 'wonder weapons' then to encourage self-delusion, no convenient buttons to be pressed in the hope of instant escape from difficulties. Each man knew that he could prevail only by his own efforts. Even in a time of widespread superstition, reliance on individual strength, courage, skill and endeavour had not yet given way to the illusion of false promise.

That assault on the psyche which is the Carnoustie effect lies in wait for those still indulging in fantasy and wishful thinking as the twentieth century, with all its manifest admonitions to realism, merges into the twenty-first.

An occasion such as the end of a century presents an opportunity to look back, to seek for clues in the conflicts of the past hundred years for the warfare to be expected during the new, the coming period.

The basic error of the twentieth century is all too easy to identify: reliance on technology to solve problems whose causes cannot be removed by technological means, since they are rooted solely in human inadequacies.

Politically, the twentieth century began as an extension of the nineteenth: the world regarded solely from national perspectives; equal enthusiasm for war on the part of the masses as well as among governments; priority given to the interests of one's own country. The peoples of Europe entered the First World War in the same confident spirit as that in which they had earlier joined the fight for or against Napoleon.

It was left to the destructive effect of modern weapons (massed artillery, machine guns, poison gas, aerial bombing) to bring about the Carnoustie effect, to put an end to the hooraying. Progress in arms development forced new attitudes to war.

As a consequence, the Second World War was joined by the next generation only reluctantly. Its outbreak inevitably stimulated weapons development further, its horrors culminating in the use of atomic bombs.

People now began to let themselves be blinded by their own technology, wavering between unrealistic expectations and exaggerated fears.

New inhibitions made their presence felt during the very next conflict, the Korean War. The *ultima ratio* was in the armoury, but no one dared to use it for fear of extending the fighting.

The world's two best-armed powers showed no such hesitation about entering wars in poor countries (Vietnam and Afghanistan), only to discover that even the greatest technological superiority was of no use to them. The two giants were defeated by under-armed, irregular resistance fighters. Each had encountered his Carnoustie.

Anxious to avoid similar fiascos in future, the Western powers tried to avoid risking any burning of their own fingers *vis-à-vis* Iraq. No more rushing in blindly, no courting any loss of international prestige. 'Hands off' was the circumlocution devised for the new, fashionable manner of solving problems by push-button – or, more accurately, for the new, fashionable path of self-deception.

Such is the lack of realistic perception accompanying the end of the twentieth century. For a long time already, man's technical knowledge has been racing ahead of his understanding of himself. Once again he is searching for a solution to international problems among his technological know-how.

Anyone capable of clear thought must look a little further. Or risk experiencing the Carnoustie effect.

Man-made problems

WHY WAR?

'From now on, war will be regarded as an obsolete anachronism, never to be revived.'
— *Herbert Asquith, formerly Prime Minister, in the House of Commons, on the announcement of the Armistice, November 11, 1918*

For every halfway-civilized human being, the reflection that warfare will have a future at all during the third millennium AD is a deeply regrettable, yet sadly unavoidable, conclusion.

Only a fool or a criminal actually *wants* war.

Yet anyone concerning himself even superficially with the history of mankind will be unable to avoid acknowledging that war is the force which has shaped our world and which continues to refashion it. As the Chinese Communist leader Mao Zedong expressed it, political power springs from the barrel of a rifle.

Admittedly, this somewhat crass formulation does little for our self-esteem as humans. We would all much rather hear that it was intellectual attainment and humane sensitivities which advanced the state of mankind. Yet in the final analysis all human endeavour, including that in pursuit of what is precious and beautiful, can take place only within the framework of the society which has been formed, and will continue to be reshaped, by an endless succession of wars. The sword giveth, and the sword taketh away.

The cycle shows no sign of coming to an end. For centuries, the pattern has been the same: two wars between states break out on average every year – not counting short-lived eruptions of cross-border fighting, revolutionary or religious wars, internal power struggles and other types of civil war. Anyone reaching down a history encyclopaedia, and taking the trouble to count, will ascertain that a good hundred wars break out worldwide in each period of fifty years. Since 1945 there have been more than 130 wars; the trend is rising rather than falling. The total number of war dead during the twentieth century is likely to have reached 100 millions.

15

We must therefore live with war, irrespective of whether we welcome the fact. We shall not be asked whether we want a war; we shall simply find ourselves in one. The only questions are when, and against whom.

Looking round the world, the ordinary citizen may well find himself unable to detect any potential enemies now that the Soviet Union has collapsed. Protests that no enemy is visible on the horizon become loudest whenever it is a question of large budget requirements for new and expensive weapons systems.

It is generally forgotten that crises necessitating the engagement of troops are almost never foreseen.

When Lord Carrington became Defence Minister in 1970, he asked his ministry officials how often British forces had been in action since 1945, and on how many of those occasions the situation had been anticipated. He was told that there had been forty-two instances of action for our men in that period – and that only three of these emergencies had been foreseen.

In other words, during all the upheavals of the years between 1945 and 1970, with a quarter century of nuclear arms race, the 'Cold War' between East and West, dissolution of the British Empire and all the other massive changes to the map of the world – during those twenty-five years of the most highly visible international tensions – the experts of one of the most heavily engaged powers were able to anticipate no more than every fourteenth event making necessary the despatch of troops into combat.

By 1999, the number of conflicts in which British forces had been engaged since 1945 had climbed to no fewer than seventy-one.

However strong may be the wish for permanent peace, how can anyone assume that there will be no further occasion for being thankful for possessing the most modern weapons and well-trained soldiers? What statesman could accept the responsibility of allowing his nation to be anything other than highly armed at all times?

Admittedly, war has long since become obsolescent as an instrument of state policy. In a world which has generally recognized that the interests of all peoples are closely dependent on one another and that these interests are best served by means of concession and co-operation, there is no room for any approach encompassing advancement of one's own interests by means of force. So at least is the theory. Unfortunately for suffering humanity, this necessary insight has not yet penetrated everywhere. The Second World War was concluded with attempts at Nuremberg and Tokyo finally to condemn the waging of aggressive war as a crime and so gradually to eliminate it from international life.

Despite these efforts, there has since then been no single day on which there has not been fighting somewhere on earth.

Currently there are some thirty wars in progress. This fact alone illustrates how far we are from an age in which there may be peace all over the world for 365 days in the year. The very first day on which there is no fighting anywhere on earth for an entire twenty-four hours will have to be regarded as the most significant milestone so far in the progress of the human race – and mankind would seem to be as far away as ever from even this modest single day.

Expectations will have to be lowered. The dream of worldwide, lasting peace must be abandoned as unattainable. Fantasies are to be laid aside and replaced by achievable objectives.

Realistically attainable aims can be no higher than:
   doing one's best to prevent the outbreak of war;
   when war nonetheless erupts, waging it in such a way that it can be concluded and survived with a minimum of human suffering;
   concluding peace in such a just manner that there can be no excuse for renewed military action.

Realizing even these more achievable aims will require a greater sense of realism than has hitherto been apparent in international affairs. It will demand not just a high degree of diplomatic skill, but also increased preparedness to preserve peace through credible deterrence. Such a rational attitude is the direct antithesis of the unreal 'pacifist' policies of the disarmers, and a confirmation of the ancient saying *'Si vis pacem, para bellum'* (If you want peace, prepare for war). This maxim has lost none of its validity with time, and is unlikely to do so. Equal attention should nonetheless be paid to that alternative golden rule suggested by the great military theoretician Sir Basil Liddell Hart: 'If you want peace, *understand* war'. There can be no hope at all of progress without making some sort of an effort along these lines.

According to Plato, writing nearly 400 years before Christ, Socrates urged that children should be taken into the field with armies, so that they could watch battles. They should, he said, be taken on horseback *'close up, to be given a taste of blood'*. The intention was to prepare children for adult life, just as they would naturally be given opportunity to observe any trade or craft before being called on to learn it themselves. It was argued that the risk to children as spectators would be outweighed by the improvement in their adult performances accruing from early familiarity with war. Here was a conscious attempt, by means of a kind of 'work experience' programme, to avoid the Carnoustie effect when reality was encountered.

In much of today's world, children do not need to be taken to watch battles; war comes to them all too readily. The ancient Greek philosophers might reasonably have expected there to be great advances in human conduct during the course of the next 24 centuries. As we see only too clearly, this has not been the case, with even the most advanced countries sometimes abandoning humane and just laws and practices which had enjoyed both validity and observance in the ancient world.

There can be no room for self-delusion about this: that as long as the human race endures, we shall be unable to eliminate the use of force. Life without violence is as unthinkable as life without illness. Every course of action proceeding from any other assumption bears within it the seeds of its own failure.

Observation shows that while the technology developed by man improves rapidly, the basic nature of man himself is not developing any further at all. While man is thoroughly capable of thinking coolly, objectively and logically when dealing with inanimate objects or materials, as well as in abstract and scientific reasonings, he only rarely displays any cool detachment in his dealings with his fellows. On the contrary, the course of human relationships is dictated almost exclusively by purely emotional perceptions.

Man has, for example, proved capable of landing on the moon at the exactly planned minute in the precisely calculated place, and of returning to earth with the same accuracy. Despite this, his day-to-day dealings with his fellow-humans are still governed by the consequences of his unreasoned actions, dictated by emotions and instinctive drives.

This contradistinction between scientific ability and social incompetence is the source of all human tragedy. Whether in a matter of simple personal interaction or in dealings between nation states, that rationality which has so proved its worth in abstract and technical questions is usually left behind, while free rein is given to more or less primitive upsurges of emotion. The greatest, most gifted, coolest of analytical research scientists can act like a totally irrational oaf when at home among his wife and children.

There is, of course, a simple reason for this. Mathematical calculations, scientific researches or abstract reasonings do not directly stimulate our emotions, unless perhaps annoyance with ourselves at being unable to find a solution. We do not normally experience anger, for instance, when contemplating a sequence of numbers. The actions of our fellows – and sometimes even the mere presence or just the thought of them – can on the other hand excite quite powerful reactions in us. It is the upsurge of these feelings which appears to release what one might generically call reason-inhibiting substances in the brain. Under the influence of our emotions, the mind can no longer perform with its accustomed objectivity and precision. It becomes as useful as a typewriter whose keys are randomly connected to all the wrong letters – and which mysteriously activate a different one each time they are struck.

Emotion is the enemy of thought. Anyone unaware of the destructive effects of feelings on our reasoning behaviour has only to observe individuals in the crowd at an important football match. He will see gestures, hear language and experience abandonment of reasoned argument and judgement such as will, if he is not himself equally primitive, make him doubt the sanity of his fellows. Yet most of those behaving in a manner calculated to make one fear for the future of the species are likely to create a favourably normal impression if encountered away from the emotional atmosphere of conflict. Perfectly decent fellows every day, no doubt, yet crazed animals once their sensibilities and loyalties are aroused.

Even when passions are not obviously stirred, our greatest inhibition to reason stems from an inbuilt resistance to accept and to take into consideration facts which do not concur with the picture which we prefer to maintain in our minds. This we might call *antignosis* – hostility to knowing – as opposed to the more familiar *diagnosis*, or investigation [Greek gnosis – knowing].

Antignosis, rejection of knowledge which we find unpleasant, is the refuge of the closed mind and the foe of rational analysis.

Aside from any question of not wanting to know, too many people simply do not bother to give themselves the opportunity to find out, let alone to sit down and think. They fill the space between their ears with noise, instead of knowledge, and are too busy talking to sit quietly and evaluate. Challenging people to think remains an unwelcome undertaking, given the natural human preference for having our senses excited rather than our minds set to work.

Yet there is a great deal of good common sense among the general public, and most people prove mentally nimble enough when it comes to devising excuses to cover their own weakness and shifting the blame elsewhere. We can think all right, once stimulated or compelled by circumstance to do so. The difficulty appears to arise from a reluctance to make the effort, compounded in an age of instant news reporting by the misleading effect of the sheer mass of information of a superficial character which is flung at the public daily. This tends to make people imagine that they already know enough of the world and are abreast of its problems. Ask them to write down a comprehensive analysis of a given topic, and this illusion is quickly shattered. No thanks accrue, of course, for exposing another's ignorance.

Clearly, any efforts at preserving peace must mean respecting sensibilities which can stimulate bellicose reactions. Such an ancient, fundamental rule of diplomacy and statecraft, one might think, scarcely requires to be stated. Sadly, it is a lesson which continually needs to be learned anew.

Yet why do human beings fight at all? Why do the smallest setbacks or difficulties trigger off in so many people not a determination to find a rational solution, but an immediate aggressive reaction? It is essential to look squarely and unflinchingly at unflattering facts about ourselves.

Long before man had learned to cultivate his own food supply – an ability which enabled him to settle in one place – his life consisted almost exclusively of one continual search for what was edible. In this permanent struggle to survive, he was merely one more living creature among many others. Early man was frequently forced to fight for what he needed against other creatures – including his fellow-humans – who were similarly struggling for nourishment.

In this competition, certain characteristics specific to man must have contributed to the development of his advanced level of fighting spirit. As with all the higher forms of life, the instinct for survival does not stop with the individual alone. There is an at least equal drive to preserve the lives of progeny and – *vis-à-vis* other species – of other members of humankind. This concern for the preservation of the species *per se* is preprogrammed into man's genes. Human progeny remain weak and defenceless for a much longer period than those of any other form of life. While the young of most animal species can be left to fend for themselves reasonably quickly, human offspring need the protection of their parents for several years. Early man was forced to defend from the attacks of hungry, less fortunate rivals not only the food which he had found, plucked or hunted, but even his own babies and their mothers, who represented potential nourishment for the larger wild beasts.

It was possibly this very helplessness of progeny within a group which led to the first co-operative protective measures among our distant ancestors. Early man probably did not take long to discover that the group could be protected best through co-operation with his fellows. Just as men banded together for joint hunting expeditions, they will also have united when the necessity for defence arose.

These measures towards collective security probably represented the beginnings of all organized society. A consequence of co-operative food-gathering and protective measures was that it enabled human beings, alone among all animate creatures, to live on after they had become old, weak and no longer capable of fighting for, and hunting, their own food. Responsibility for the aged, along with the young, then became a further spur to organized hunting and defence.

It is apparent that in order to survive at all, early man needed to develop an automatic reaction of belligerence both to defend himself against danger and to overcome difficulties in general. In his prehistory days, man was able to secure his survival as a species only by himself becoming as aggressive a creature as his dangerous animal rivals.

Pugnacity in the face of real or imagined threats is in itself therefore nothing more nor less than both natural and healthy. Without having developed an intense fighting spirit in the early days of his emergence, man would have disappeared from the earth while still in the process of evolution. The simple fact that we humans exist today is evidence of the successfully bellicose nature developed by our ancestors when under threat. It was only this aggressive spirit which enabled man to achieve mastery over his environment and over all other forms of life.

This survival tool is only one of many basic characteristics, essential once in the early stages of our evolution, still present in our genetic composition. Yet such an advanced degree of belligerence has long since become superfluous in most people's everyday lives. Our hereditary predisposition to pugnacity, though *per se* of a positive character (because life-preserving), tends to act in a manner which is self-defeating. In all higher forms of life, not only in man, a natural egoism comes to the fore, the instinct to defend oneself, one's home, one's blood relations, the members of the group to which one belongs and the territory of that group. This instinct extends to a readiness to self-sacrifice, if necessary. In the

22

case of mankind, what is to be defended is the family, society, the nation, the homeland.

Altruism and egoism exist side-by-side in human nature – with even the altruism serving a selfish interest, if not for the individual, then at least for the preservation of the species as a whole. Our distant ancestors will have discovered at an early stage that the group functions better – that is, has greater chances of survival – if the individual sacrifices himself when necessary for the benefit of others.

Humans have no bodily weapons for their defence: no large, sharp teeth, no claws, no hooves. Nor are rabbits blessed with weapons. The individual rabbit saves himself by swift flight until he can go to cover underground; he secures the continuation of his species by liberal propagation of his genes. These two characteristics, speed and fertility, are embedded genetically in the rabbit as a dual defence system to thwart extinction.

Like the rabbit, man has his own ways of compensating for his lack of bodily weapons in safeguarding not only his individual survival but also that of his species. Man too makes use of that particular attribute in which he is superior to his enemies: his brain. His capacity for analytical thought, his imagination and his gift for improvization are for man what legs and reproductive organs are for the rabbit.

Man differs from the animal world which surrounds him in one important respect. All creatures have in common that they defend what is material, including life itself. Man alone enjoys a world of ideas as well as one of material existence, and consequently is the only living being prepared to fight for a belief.

Many creatures are able to some extent to communicate feelings, impressions, needs and warnings to their fellows. Only man has developed a language which enables him to communicate thoughts, ideas and memories as well. He alone has also produced writing, allowing him to convey memories and the products of his imagination and reasoning to persons well out of his personal physical reach, to people in other parts of the world and even to those in later ages. Our unique ability imposes a duty on us to learn from this store of experience and knowledge and to think before we act.

The first duty of the state is the protection of its citizens. Self-defence requires neither explanation nor justification. At the same time, there is sadly no shortage of cases in which a supposedly preventive or defensive war has been opened unnecessarily out of unjustified fear of a supposed threat.

Before undertaking hostilities, it is essential to be absolutely clear what are the values which it is felt necessary to defend. At various times and in differing societies, diverse values have been felt to be worth defending with the sacrifice of life itself: a tribe, a belief, a ruler, a dynasty, a state, material parity, personal or national liberty. Wars are, however, not fought only to defend such values, but also to propagate their influence and to extend spheres of power.

Unquestionably, most people involved in all such campaigns believe in the justice of their cause. Yet nearly all wars have their origins not in virtuous intentions but in those same inadequacies of human nature which can be noted every day in dealings with one's fellows.

It is unnecessary to live through a war in order to observe these disastrous flaws in mankind. They can be recognized most clearly in everyday road traffic, above all:

an incapacity to think more than one step in advance;
an unwillingness to put oneself in the other fellow's position;
the attitude that only 'I' count – a behavioural defect revealing a fundamental contempt for others and confirming what remains of the primitive wild creature in man.

Commonplace egoistic disregard of the rights and needs of others, this remainder from the prehistory days of permanent struggle for naked survival, is the wellspring of bad (and dangerous) behaviour on the roads, just as it is of robbery with violence, rape or war.

This contempt for others and its root, egoism, are what make greed the commonest cause of war. Ambitious striving to make life better and more secure is healthy; its mutation, greed, is on the other hand deeply unhealthy. Anything which promotes the interests of some while damaging those of others does not advance mankind, but sets it back as a society and as a species.

Yes, the individual has to survive. But no, he does not need to hurt others in order to do so.

Humankind can be observed to divide naturally into two distinct, contrasting types of individual. There are those who use any superior strength or position which they might enjoy to take advantage of those weaker than themselves. There are also those in whom recognition of another's weakness inspires the impulse to protect, not to exploit. This, fundamentally, is the distinction marking out the developmentally retarded from the truly advanced specimen of what, in our conceit, we call *homo sapiens*. It is not a division separating nation from nation, but only one between individuals. Like all such attributes constituting the emotional disposition or character of the individual, these diverging attitudes to one's fellows have no discernible direct relationship to intelligence or to other personal qualities.

Much of humankind's suffering originates in, or is at least compounded by, our individual and collective over-evaluation of ourselves. We are the masters of the universe. We can do wonderful things. Yes, we can. We also behave, on the least provocation, as though there is a component missing somewhere in our brains. It is time to stop being so damned conceited and to realize that man is an incomplete being. If we look honestly at the succession of our own actions and reactions, we are compelled to acknowledge that it is a tightrope walk that we perform, needing only a very small push to bring us down from rationality to irrationality. At times we can all behave as though we should more accurately call ourselves *homo idioticus*, if not *homo bestialis*.

Whatever beliefs many people may hold about humanity's being an élite divine creation, the only safe approach, both to ourselves and to our fellows, is to regard man as simply a highly evolved mammal who has developed both manual dexterity and the faculty of speech. Witnessing how man abuses these abilities to hurt his fellows ought to bring us down to earth pretty sharply. Certainly we can observe mammals 'lower' than ourselves behaving incomparably better towards one another than do most humans. Of ourselves, it is always wiser to expect too little, rather than too much.

If we really want to put an end to the recurrence of our self-inflicted difficulties, we can allow no room for illusions and conceit. It is essential to ignore the politician's waffle, to recognize what is mere propaganda and to disregard whatever people want us to believe which contradicts the evidence of our own senses and experience. As the Perth whisky distiller Thomas Dewar warned so accurately:

'Minds are like parachutes. They work only when they are open.'

Our mental posture must be that of a man with feet planted securely on firm ground, his head kept high – not in the clouds, but held up to face fearlessly whatever lies before him, his clear eyes focused solely on unambiguous facts. To lose contact with reality is to squander that most precious of all gifts with which we have been endowed: our under-used capacity for lucid thought.

Each of us has only one relatively brief span of life. It is our attitude to the question how we wish to use this time which demonstrates either our individual worth or our worthlessness. If we are simply to exist, to eat, to procreate, to serve only our own ends until we die, then we remain indistinguishable from those other creatures to whom we, unjustifiably, feel superior. If, on the other hand, each of us makes a conscious effort to attain a progressively higher standard of personal conduct as we go through life, then mankind as a whole will be advanced. Sadly, experience seems to indicate that periods of stable and selfless society endure for only a generation or two. Selfish materialism, such as we have seen devouring the world during the latter half of the twentieth century, makes short work of ideals and sets back humanity very rapidly.

Living life merely for one's own gratification and gain may be enjoyable for the individual; it is also pointless and has nothing but negative consequences for mankind *in toto*. A nation in which such attitudes are widespread will be found incapable of prevailing in war.

An over-reaction to perceived danger still causes humanity a very great deal of unnecessary suffering. The natural instinct for hitting back in order to ensure survival is not infrequently the determining impulse in undertaking the step into war – often quite needlessly.

Everyone will be familiar with the dog which unleashes a menacing barrage of barking at even the most peaceful of passers-by, in an effort to warn off any supposed assaults on 'its' territory, the home of the family to which it belongs. Even after years of experience have shown the beast that in practice no one e ver actually attempts to occupy 'its' house and garden, the dog still cannot change its behaviour. The instinct to adopt a threatening, aggressive stance at even the least suggestion of a threat to the basis of its existence is born into the dog, programmed into its genes. The fact that it still barks, even when it knows that this is pointless, is evidence of the triumph of thoughtless instinct over the analytical functions of the brain.

In the course of a seven-digit number of years, the dog has admittedly evolved a quite long way. All the same, it is unable to free itself from certain indispensable innate characteristics developed to ensure its own preservation.

Humans have in their genes this same natural instinct to defend themselves and whatever they regard as their own. If man wishes to be a human being, and not an animal, he must always strive, unlike the dog, to keep his feelings, his instincts and his upsurges of emotion under the control of his thoughts. Emotions can stimulate both thought and action, but all too frequently they prevent accurate working of the brain.

The dog is unable to raise himself above the level of its genetic predispositions; man should at least make an effort to do so. Man must not allow himself to be ruled by his emotions; on the contrary, he must use that one tool which he has, his brain, to rule these very emotions. It will be clear to all that certain people and groups of people have evolved this capacity for self-control to a significantly higher degree than others.

Crime is chiefly a matter for adolescent and maturing youth. To some extent, delinquent behaviour can be a symptom of an attempt to prove or to assert the growing personality, a first step along the road to making one's own decisions and determining one's own actions, free from the supervision and restraint of parents. Whereas most people pass beyond this stage and have little difficulty in becoming responsible and considerate citizens, a minority remains inwardly permanently immature and inclined to criminal behaviour even into later years. Young states, whether new configurations, freshly independent former colonies or post-revolutionary creations, display the same urge of the immature youngster to test the limits of their capabilities. The first decades of newly-won freedom for these states are frequently characterized by attempts to take territory from their nearest neighbours.

Nearly every living creature exists under permanent threat from a predator specific to its genus. The natural predator to man is man himself.

The immoral shark of the business world who drives his rivals into bankruptcy or swallows them, in order to become sole ruler of his field, is animated by the same predatory impetus which drives the national leader wanting to extend his territory by conquering his neighbours. The continual reappearance on the scene of just such a figure would seem to be as unavoidable a phenomenon in human affairs as rain or snow in meteorology.

As history shows, advanced societies and peoples are repeatedly attacked by less developed ones. At first sight, this might appear to constitute an argument for delivering the speediest and most generous development aid possible, so that all peoples and countries on earth might soon be on the same economic level. Yet material equality has little to do with willingness to live in peace with neighbouring peoples. The most destructive wars are fought out between nations enjoying comparable economic prosperity.

Animals kill principally in order to eat, that is, out of necessity. No species of animal mistreats its fellows in the merciless fashion practised by humans. Such cruelty is raised to its pinnacle whenever an attempt is made to convince others of the rightness of an idea.

Wars of religion or ideology – of belief – are conducted in a significantly crueller fashion than straightforward wars for the expansion of power or economic position. The Christian Crusades, the wars to spread Islam, the Thirty Years' War and the Second World War were all characterized by uninhibited cruelty and a lack of chivalry. Civil wars tend to be fought in nearly as ruthless a fashion as such wars of belief. To kill for food is to obey the laws of nature; to kill because someone does not share an idea or a faith of ours is to pervert those abilities with which nature has endowed us.

Whereas the more advanced nations are gradually abandoning war against one another, less developed peoples are waging more wars than ever.

It is not massive wars between industrial nations which must be expected in the early twenty-first century, but the increasing necessity for intervention by the armed forces of these nations, to put an end to wars between developing peoples.

We are not moving towards a world without war, but towards a world in which the centre of gravity of warfare has shifted, both ethnically and geographically.

PEACE FOR WHOSE TIME?

In the course of the twentieth century, mankind took the most significant step forward in its long history: somewhere around mid-century, the leading nations – even though in many cases reluctantly – began to accept that war was no longer worthwhile.

Despite this apparent prospect of progress, the twenty-first century now beginning will be characterized by wars started by less advanced peoples, which to a greater or lesser extent will also affect the older established nations.

A widely believed legend holds that one solitary work of mankind is visible from space: the Great Wall of China, erected to protect the Chinese from the recurring attacks of hordes from Central Asia (Mongols, Turks, Huns). Astronauts dismiss this claim, denying that even such a gigantic structure can be seen from space. Today's experts even question whether the Great Wall ever really was intended to keep the Mongols and other peoples at bay. Whatever the facts, there is a certain wry fascination in the reflection that of all the achievements of man's long history a military construction might be the first evidence of mankind seen by an approaching alien – testimony to the innate predator in man. This unflattering image of mankind obliges us to adopt an honest and fearless approach to the entire question of war and the preservation of peace.

We are handicapped in such efforts by the limits imposed on our knowledge thanks to the way in which most history is written. Reading popular history books can be a noisy business; one is practically deafened by the sound of axes being ground. The original Greek word, *historia*, does not mean a narrative, but an inquiry. Sadly, almost no history is written in a spirit of inquiry; the motive appears usually to be protection or enhancement of the reputation of one or more protagonists.

If sport were to be reported as most history is recorded, a football team, for example, would have its own goals described and praised, with those of its opponents not being mentioned. An instance is provided by England's first match after having collected the 1966

World Cup. With historians on the job, the home team's next Wembley encounter (England 2; Scotland 3) would by now be 'remembered' by everyone as an England victory.

In sport, fortunately, specific reality is recorded; history is almost exclusively a field for subjective, and selective, interpretation.

Half-truths and suppression of facts are of course lying. Avoiding what we find uncomfortable, retreating into wishful thinking, will do nothing to free man from the cycle of his ever-recurring suffering. We must not be afraid to acknowledge honestly our own inadequacies, or fear, in researching and expressing what is demonstrably true, to give offence. Evasiveness is the stuff of politics; it can never be a resort for the serious mind. Only an uncompromising readiness to call spades spades can advance mankind – presupposing, of course, an ability to recognize spades in the first place. Conflicts, whether between individuals or between nations, frequently originate in mistaken perceptions. We misjudge the other fellow's intentions, overestimate his power to harm us and – as often as not – miscalculate our own capacity to put things right (as we see them).

Common or garden human idiocy is at the back of most trouble. It is worth sparing a few minutes to reflect on how we, and our political leaders, make our frequently fatal decisions.

Subconscious acts derive from instincts and reflex reactions, and can scarcely be governed. Every conscious act, on the other hand, results from a decision of will, for which the individual can be called to account. Whether in petty matters or in grave ones, decisions to act are driven by motivations from two sources: perception and emotion. Our emotions arise partly from instincts, partly from our experiences and partly from individual temperament. They influence our interpretation of, and reactions to, what we perceive. It is in the realm of our perceptions that the greatest follies can be committed. Ideally, all of our view of a situation should be based on *knowledge*, that is, on ascertainable, unquestionable fact. In practice, this is almost never possible. We are forced to complement verifiable knowledge by relying on *assumptions*, on what we calculate to be the case. Clearly, the degree of accuracy of all assessments will be in direct proportion to both the amount of determinable information available and our skill in evaluating and interpreting this – assuming willingness on the part of the individual even to attempt objective analysis. After this, the problems multiply. The sum of our *knowledge* and *assumptions*, which we regard as our understanding of the situation, then becomes subject to our *prejudices* about the protagonists, any religious, ideological or personal *convictions* to which we may adhere, our capacity for *self-delusion* and to the sum of the *emotions* roused, including the reaction of our *instincts*.

What we *feel*, what we *think* that we know, what we manage to *persuade ourselves* are the facts of the matter – these are what determine our actions and reactions. Nothing is of less relevance in human behaviour than the facts. It is ignorance and wishful thinking which make the world go round, not love of truth. The voice which we obey is the one telling us what we want to believe.

It is curious that while most people are to some degree concerned with their bodily health and fitness, few bother even to consider the need for soundness of thought. It is not difficult to convince people of the wisdom of avoiding ruining their bodies with an intake of what has come to be called 'junk food', yet they will readily fill their heads with junk information from television and newspapers, and take it to be an adequate diet. It is not hard for the individual to recognize his own physical deterioration through lack of exercise, but he will see no necessity for attaining mental fitness through the discipline of probing research and analytical reasoning. Mention that he is overweight, and generally he will acknowledge his lack of fitness in good part. Suggest that his preference for being entertained rather than thinking has made him mentally unfit, and he will feel insulted in the extreme.

While admittedly there is no shortage of people who have little to offer apart from their bodies and what they can do with them, what distinguishes man from his fellow-creatures is that besides a body he also possesses a mind. Man's commonplace error is to take his mind for granted, to assume that the first thing that comes into his head is always going to be the right answer. Whereas the only valid view is one arising from logical evaluation of a sum of knowledge, almost everyone will already have an opinion ready to hand, however unacquainted with the subject.

Knowledge has to come before opinion; without knowledge, no one is even *entitled* to hold an opinion. We are continually faced with questions to which the only honest answer that we can give is 'I don't know', or at the very least 'I don't know enough'. Yet how infrequently will anyone admit this! No one can be blamed for having been misled by the popular media or by his upbringing, but with a little mental effort he can always find out more for himself. As the great Liddell Hart once put it: *'There is no excuse for any literate person to be less than three thousand years old in mind'*.

It is part of man's perpetual self-delusion to overestimate his grasp of any situation. Politicians, of course, as they are keen to demonstrate to us at every opportunity, already know it all, and so have no need to learn. Never are they unable to answer a question, never in need of time to work things out. This is the most dangerous mental attitude of all, a time bomb programmed not just for self-destruction, but for the destruction of others, too. Any human being who, politician-like, is not prepared to say 'I don't know', and to withhold action until he does know, is both dangerous and untrustworthy. Adding to this general peril are the adherents of mankind's multiple religious creeds, each of which is, of course, the only true faith.

We may tell ourselves that we act out of reason, and in the simplest of daily activities we may well do so. When graver, long-term decisions have to be taken, our actions are the product, in varying degrees, of *knowledge, assumption, prejudice, conviction, self-delusion, emotion* and *instinct*. Our first concern should always be to amass as great an amount as possible of *knowledge* – ascertainable facts – about the situation; our second to suppress our *prejudices*, which, like coloured spectacles, prevent accurate vision by filtering out constituent elements of the scene before these can reach the brain. Prejudice is antignosis at work, and it has no place in military assessments. The *emotions* of which we should be most wary are of course fear and anger, both of which lead all too swiftly to precipitate and unconsidered action.

Freed from the corrupting influence of emotion, the brain can be relied on to produce a situation analysis of an accuracy in direct proportion to the volume and quality of the information fed in. This of course presupposes the discarding of the filters and distorting lenses of prejudice. Sadly, most people are simply unwilling to allow the brain to function in this unhindered fashion. They appear to regard any suggestion that they should subdue or abandon their pet hatreds and favouritisms as tantamount to asking for permission to remove the sunshine from their sky.

Except in the case of the most exceptional spirits, engagement in politics serves only to polarize and intensify the individual's prejudices. The commitment of the politician's personal position, once adopted in public, makes him fear to tolerate any deviation, let alone admit error. The familiar know-it-all pigheadedness, so easily mistaken by himself for strength, merely confirms how thoroughly what he has of a mind has become closed to reason.

Even though we of this present, fortunate generation might be experiencing the end of senseless mutual slaughter and mutilation between the more advanced peoples, there is still no end in sight to the self-inflicted suffering endured by much of humankind.

Régimes which suppress opposition voices, dictatorships and one-party states, irrespective of their political colour – in short, all countries which we should not classify as 'free democracies' – these are the ones which tend towards assaults on their neighbours. Their leaders are used to having their own way in everything, resent deeply any frustration and simply crush any resistance. However poor the quality of democratic politicians, we can at least hope that a government whose members are accustomed to decide disputes by means of parliamentary cut-and-thrust will be more prepared to settle international questions by negotiation. We have the consequences of stupidity and shortsightedness to fear from our leaders, but not usually those of bloodthirstiness.

Certainly there are exceptions here; all the same, the above rule of thumb gives some idea from which quarters future breaches of international peace may be expected. It is the industrial nations, those very peoples who have given the rest of mankind its present technology, who have also developed the highest sense of care and just treatment of their suffering fellow-humans. These humane values – visible in forms of government and of justice systems – have chiefly gone out to the world from Europe. Today the more advanced standards are embraced by North America and by countries such as Australia and New Zealand, whereas paradoxically no common level has yet been attained throughout Europe itself (one need only compare the differing treatment given to accused persons arrested in, for example, Norway and Serbia).

It is principally Europe and North America which have led the world into the era of sophisticated scientific achievement – and who will be forced to defend themselves against the applications of this same technology. The victors of the Second World War were the first to arm themselves with nuclear weapons. As is well known, eight states from within that former alliance possess nuclear arsenals openly: the United States, the UK, France, China, Russia, the Ukraine, Belarus and Kazakhstan – the last-named four as former member states of the USSR.

From the very beginning, it was as certain as the succession of night and day that membership of the atomic club was not going to remain confined to these founders. It is an open secret that Israel, surrounded as she is by arch-enemies, has possessed a nuclear arsenal for many years. South Africa, which for long felt similarly threatened by her neighbours, built six nuclear bombs during the 1970s, but dismantled them during 1990-91. Apart from these two countries, it tends to be the leaders of peoples with a low standard of living and a neglect of human rights who make the strongest efforts to be able to strut on the world stage as nuclear 'powers'.

That giant land of poverty, India (annual income per capita 330 US dollars; illiteracy rate fifty-two per cent), detonated an atomic bomb as early as 1974. In May 1998, India conducted a series of underground nuclear explosions. The fact that the site chosen for these tests was less than five miles from inhabited villages raises justified questions about the fitness of an Indian government to be in possession of such weapons at all. In 1994, a former member of the Pakistan government admitted publicly that his country, too (annual income per capita 400 US dollars; illiteracy rate sixty-five per cent), possessed a nuclear arsenal. Though this confession was later denied by Prime Minister Benazir Bhutto, Pakistan was nonetheless able to respond to India's series of tests in May 1998 with a similar succession of underground detonations of her own. Three times since the foundation of the two states in 1947, India and Pakistan have waged war over possession of the disputed province of Kashmir. Now both governments aver that they want to have nuclear weapons solely for their own protection. Time will tell.

It is no secret that Iraq, Iran, North Korea and Libya are all conducting their own nuclear weapons programmes. Despite a treaty concluded in 1967, designating Latin America a 'nuclear-free zone', both Argentina and Brazil initiated nuclear weapons programmes during the 1970s, though each is now supposed to have abandoned these efforts.

One hundred and eighty-seven states have signed the Nuclear Non-Proliferation Treaty, pledging themselves to abstain from acquiring atomic weapons. These states concluded an agreement at the United Nations in May 2000 to strive for abolition of all nuclear arms. Even the nuclear 'big five', the USA, Russia, China, Britain and France, found themselves undertaking to abolish their own nuclear arsenals – without of course committing themselves to any timetable for doing so. Despite the expressed intentions of the states concerned, it is certain that the number of nuclear-armed states will increase early in the twenty-first century. Not every nation acquiring atomic weapons will be animated by the same regard for preserving peace and for maintaining human rights as are the industrial peoples of Europe and North America. Even so, nuclear arms will raise their possessor to a position of influence which cannot be ignored, at least within their own immediate region of the world.

Of course, possession of nuclear weapons will not by itself enable an assault on an industrial nation. A nuclear warhead must also be delivered to its objective. A state in the Middle East or Africa succeeding in building nuclear weapons will also be concerned to develop means of conveying these to their targets – not excluding terrorist methods. It must be assumed that even the sophisticated defence systems of an advanced industrial state can be overcome once or even several times by means of a surprise attack. Industrial nations will naturally be able to answer nuclear attacks successfully, but all the same, the human loss and material damage sustained is likely to be horrendous. Thanks to developments in rocket technology, any nation, however safe it may feel, is effectively being drawn within range of, for example, a developing country led by religious fanatics. Twelve countries already possess rocket systems. Chemical, biological or nuclear weapons programmes are being pursued by a total of twenty-five states.

Modern technology, complete industries and weapons are supplied to developing nations, many of whose young people are trained as engineers and technicians at universities and technical institutes in industrial countries. These fledglings return to their homelands to help form the development of the societies emerging there, taking their freshly acquired technical knowledge home. What they cannot take with them are those humane values which the ancient European peoples have learned painfully in the course of thousands of years. It is, indeed, unreasonable to expect them to be able to do so. The leap from a straw hut to an atomic power station might be achieved within a single generation, but the transition from witch doctor divination to the reasoned judgement of a wise, objective and far-seeing humanist can on the other hand be completed only through the collective experiences of several millennia.

After the trauma inflicted on the intellect by the experience of Hitler's attempts to wipe out European Jewry, it is nothing less than natural that civilized minds should reject any attempts to discriminate negatively between races and nations. The temptation, in reaction to the horrors of the extermination camps, is to tell oneself rigidly to regard all human life as one and the same.

For legal and humanitarian purposes, this is unquestionably the correct approach. All people should enjoy both equal rights and equal responsibilities under the law, as well as receiving the same humanitarian considerations. Any other attitude will inevitably lead to errors of individual judgement and ultimately to disaster.

Rights to humane and just treatment are not dependent on personal qualities, nor do they presuppose any equivalence in these. Individuals, and groups of individuals, vary widely in their capabilities, their temperaments and their behaviour patterns. It is these divergences which have to be taken into account; to ignore them risks potentially fatal errors in responding to other people's actions.

While we ourselves should always strive to treat all fellow-creatures with equal humanity, it would be foolish to expect the same in return, to forget, for example, the treatments dealt to prisoners of war in the Far East and to helpless civilian populations in Africa. In defence matters it is imperative to interpret accurately the character of both enemies and allies, actual and potential. There is no merit in refusing to acknowledge what we do not wish to see, any more than in failing to evaluate recognizable characteristics.

In their silly and superficial way, people engaged in politics and others obsessed with dictating public thought have trivilialized the matter by reducing it to an issue of skin colour. You and I, dear reader, would remain the same persons even were some freak biological process to transform our epidermal pigmentation. Had we, on the other hand, been born of other racial stock, then our personalities would be different from their present composition, this book would not exist and you would perhaps not be interested in reading about the subject, anyway.

Our minds are there to be used, for collection of data as well as for analysis. The essential point to remember is that no nation has an exclusive monopoly of either genius or stupidity, of humanity any more than of cruelty. Every country has its share of admirable as well as of despicable elements. What varies from one situation to the next is which constituents are currently in control of a state.

In Europe it has taken thousands of years to arrive at a willingness among the diverse nations to live together peacefully in a spirit of harmonious co-operation. Even now not all the peoples living on the soil of Europe have reached the same stage. Most nations around the world have still to make this journey of development, and it is certain that not all will achieve the same level of maturity.

The outward forms of democracy may be imposed on, or adopted by, young states. The limited extent to which true democratic values and behaviour have become absorbed by the peoples concerned is confirmed by recurrent news reports of brutal intimidation of voters in former colonies, of the ignoring of referendum results and even of situations where a government refuses to acknowledge victory by another party in an election as a reason to hand over power.

Dealing with inanimate materials can be taught; the imparting of humane values is frequently thwarted by ancient, ingrained callousness, an indifference to the suffering of others.

This is certainly not to say that all the peoples of less developed countries are equally backward or unfeeling in their treatment of their fellows. On the contrary, many who to us might appear materially primitive are completely peaceable and demonstrate the tenderest love and consideration towards each other. Possibly it is precisely the lack of material possessions, coupled with the presence of adequate food supplies, which makes possible harmonious communal life without greed. Whatever the reasons, such peoples do not represent any danger even to their immediate neighbours, let alone any threat to the developed world. It is rather those nations which are already on the way to emulating the material prosperity of the industrial states who threaten to destabilize the world through their sheer greed.

The struggle to improve one's circumstances, including material ones, is of course perfectly natural. If it is possible to make people's life easier, more comfortable and safer, then the pursuit of these goals must be the natural task of any government. Such endeavours do not of themselves constitute a threat to other nations. Those who do threaten others are chiefly states whose governments disregard the human rights of their own citizens, particularly when their leaders are motivated by an intolerant religious belief or ideology.

Though many of its peoples have suffered through the tyranny, torture and mass murder of communism, Europe, except for the

Balkans, has at least been spared war since 1945. In the rest of the world, on the other hand, some twenty million people have been killed during the same period in around 130 wars – without the use of nuclear weapons. A further sixty millions have been forced to flee from their homes.

With only few exceptions, these 130 or so wars have been fought between countries of the so-called 'Third World', that is, between peoples whose societies are in a state of development well below that of the industrial nations. These peoples presumably need to undergo the same experiences and follow the same path of development as the most advanced nations have done.

The question arises whether industrial nations should intervene in such wars, in order to curtail human suffering. They certainly intervene whenever their own interests are threatened by the warfare of third parties; in other cases they content themselves with the role of outraged spectators. The Western powers intervened quickly enough in 1991, in order to liberate Kuwait from Iraqi occupation. At stake here were oil supplies from the Persian Gulf vital to the industrial nations. During this Gulf War, thirty-two other wars were raging elsewhere in the world; in none of these other cases did the industrial nations feel obliged to rush to anyone's aid.

One or two things can be predicted with at least reasonable probability: old-established democracies, or other states which have enjoyed stable government for some time, will rarely go to war against one another. On the other hand, these are the very countries which will frequently be called on to enter, and put an end to, wars started by others.

Over-population alone seems likely to make new wars practically unavoidable. At the beginning of the twentieth century, the world population totalled 1,633 millions. One hundred years later the figure is 6,228 millions – almost a quadrupling despite two world wars, an uninterrupted succession of simultaneous smaller wars, numerous attempts at genocide and permanent hunger on several continents. Each second, the world total is increased by another three lives, or more than a quarter of a million every day.

United Nations estimates foresee a world peopled by some 12,000 millions by 2060 – a doubling-up in sixty years.

Ninety per cent of this expected population increase is anticipated in developing countries. Whereas no natural rise in population is expected in Europe (on the other hand, Europeans are having to cope with a stream of immigrants from other continents which is difficult to absorb), Africa already displays an alarming annual expansion of three per cent. During the final five years of the twentieth century alone, the population of Africa rose from 720 millions to no fewer than 900 millions. By 2030, this figure is expected to have reached 1,600 millions - an increase of 116 per cent in thirty-five years. Nigeria alone is even expected to double her population within only the next twenty years.

By 2030, while Africa is more than doubling her population, an increase of around one-third is anticipated for Oceania, with a fifty per cent rise in both Asia and Latin America. China alone is expected to see a leap from 1,200 millions at the turn of the century to 1,500 millions by 2030 – 300 million more stomachs to be fed, within three decades.

During the 1990s, the number of unemployed in the developing countries climbed to some 400 millions, while the Third World's share of global gross economic product continued to shrink.

It is simply unthinkable that the pressures and clashes of interests caused by these developments will not lead to protracted warfare on the various continents. According to UN statistics, much more than one third of the world's population is already living in what are described as 'hygienically inadequate conditions'. One billion human beings can neither read nor write, while a similar total are chronically undernourished. The coming explosion in numbers can only aggravate these horrors in dramatic fashion.

Shortage of food is almost certainly the oldest of all causes of war. Nearly 3,000 years ago, Homer wrote in his *Odyssey* of

'the hungering stomach, that curse, the cause of so much suffering for mankind, which drives men even to fit out great ships and to sail across the barren seas, bringing death and destruction to their enemies'.

Each year, the world consumes 2,000,000,000 tons of food (an average of roughly two pounds weight per person per day). Simply to keep step with the increase in population, food production would need to be doubled to 4,000,000,000 tons by 2060 – which, to understate the case, seems unlikely to happen. Even if superhuman efforts and several miracles were to bring about such an increase in harvests, there would still be the same proportionate number of our fellow human beings, namely now 2,000,000,000, living in a state of permanent undernourishment. Much more than a doubling of food production will be necessary to abolish hunger – and such a target appears unattainable. Instead, it must be assumed that in the twenty-first century a significantly greater proportion of humanity will die of starvation than at present. As early as 1995, world grain reserves (stocks for the period between two harvests; in this case supplies for the period between the harvests of 1995 and 1996) had fallen to the lowest level in modern history. Naturally, any worsening of the water shortage in Africa and the Middle East will aggravate this lack of food. Anyone who has seen the pictures of starving children knows where the harvest-destroying droughts of Africa lead. No one will have any difficulty in imagining the consequences, should the loudly-proclaimed 'global warming' actually take place. Tensions have already arisen between Egypt and her southerly neighbours over the diversion of Nile waters. A further potential trouble source is the Euphrates, which flows out of Turkey through Syria and Iraq to the Persian Gulf.

It may be assumed that states or régimes which are still young are more likely to represent a threat to peace than older, stable countries. In this sense, a country must be considered 'young', however old in its boundaries and population, when basic upheavals have taken place and a new, authoritarian régime holds the reins in its hand. China is an example.

All such new actors on the world stage should, like immature teenagers kicking over the traces, be kept under strict observation. Unfortunately, there is no international mechanism for preventing or punishing international delinquency.

To unleash a war of aggression shows immaturity. Just like half-baked teenagers breaking away from the authority of their parents, the leaders of new nations or régimes frequently succumb to the temptation to test the limits of their newly acquired strengths and freedom of action. After liberation from Spanish colonial rule in 1816, the Argentinians felt themselves so strong that in the following decades they waged war on their neighbours Uruguay, Brazil and Paraguay in an attempt to take territory from Brazil and to annexe both the other countries completely. Not content with this, Argentina also made demands on Chile which all but led to another war. During all these undertakings, a succession of armed revolts continued in Argentina itself until 1880. This painfully slow birth of a new nation, sixty-four years of attacking others and of civil war-like fighting at home, is typical of the conduct and development of newly created states. Many colonial possessions attaining independence behave in a similarly bellicose fashion.

As the examples of the former multiple states Yugoslavia and USSR demonstrate, such behaviour is by no means confined to liberated colonies. Now themselves autonomous, Serbs, Armenians and Georgians have lost no time in trying to extend their own possessions by force, at the cost of their neighbours. Once they have the opportunity, revolutionary régimes similarly find no difficulty in transforming themselves into imperialists. The enthusiasts of the French Revolution wanted to spread their crusade against the rule of monarchy and aristocracy into other countries, but under Napoleon soon turned this movement into the most imperialist of all attempts at conquest and subjection. The same course was followed by the Soviet Union. Mussolini and Hitler, despite impressive initial performances at home, lost many of their foreign admirers when they too adopted an imperialist course. The communist régime in Cuba has engaged in wars not only in Latin America but in Africa too, in an attempt to turn revolution into an article for export.

Until now, the great industrial centres of North America and Europe have remained untouched by the effects of such wars. This will change once Third World countries possess weapons with which they can threaten the industrial nations, for example when

Iran, Libya or Iraq acquires long-range missiles. Europe, Canada and the United States are equipped with sophisticated defence systems, but, of course, there is fallibility in everything. In the main, industrial nations will be able to ward off such assaults, but even a single nuclear weapon penetrating defences is capable of exacting a massive human and material cost. The effects of a chemical warhead in a large conurbation are equally obvious.

The yearning for worldwide peace is universal and completely natural. Britain's Prime Minister Neville Chamberlain was surely doing nothing other than expressing the general hope when he spoke during the Sudeten crisis in 1938 of *'peace for our time'*. Chamberlain told the newsreel cameras:

'War is a dreadful thing, and before we undertake it we must be very sure that it really is the great values which are at stake'.

Peace, however, requires the consent of all parties, while for war it is necessary only for a single state to break ranks. Short-term peace may be leased at any time by giving way. The snag is that meeting someone halfway and doing nothing only encourages the leader who is threatening aggression. All experience shows that aggressors must be stopped as early in their careers as possible; otherwise each success only spurs them on to further adventures.

Peace in the simple dictionary sense, that states are at the moment not actually firing at one another with live ammunition, is not enough for mankind, if man really wishes to progress. Further human development demands no abandonment of the essential triad: peace with freedom and justice. After the First World War, the League of Nations was founded with the aim of maintaining peace between states, particularly in Europe. 'No more war' was the commonest, and most understandable, slogan of those years. Yet this unquestionably noble aspiration was founded on a house of sand: the treaties of Versailles and Saint-Germain made nonsense of the League of Nations from the start. The League was condemned to fail in its object of preserving peace not because, for example, it did not possess the military 'teeth' to implement its will, but simply because it was founded to uphold a structure of states and national boundaries which was patently unjust. This was wrong and a preprogrammed disaster. It is alarming that none of the statesmen involved seems to have perceived the only sensible sequence of action: first to arrange a *just* peace and *only then* to found an international police force.

One of the signatories at Versailles, Britain's Prime Minister David Lloyd George, did complain that, for example, two million Germans had been placed under the rule of Poles and three and a half million more under that of Czechs, both of whom Lloyd George described as *'people who have never previously set up a stable government for themselves'*. As he explained, Lloyd George could not *'conceive of any greater cause of future war'* than the stripping away of German territories and *'large masses of Germans clamouring for reunion with their native land'*.

It must be apparent to all that a police force which is founded to uphold repressive and unjust legislation will inevitably forfeit the support of the citizenry and run into resistance. In the long term, only an equitable legal system can be respected. States and entire peoples do not react any differently from the individual citizen at home. They rebel against unjust treatment.

The principle of self-determination has validity in international relations, as does a further principle, that force may be used to an appropriate degree in order to restore legality. Yet most wars cause more damage and suffering than the original *casus belli*. Violence inevitably incites retaliation, while perceived threats to third party interests draw in fresh belligerents and multiply the extent and effects of the quarrel.

It may appear that the decisions and actions of the statesmen involved determine the course of events, yet in practice matters have already developed their own momentum before hostilities are opened, and can no longer be stopped or given a new direction. That the course of a war is directed by the governments involved is true only to a limited extent; such a belief is largely a matter of self-deception. This fact underlines the necessity of finding a solution to existing or looming problems before the stage is reached at which control over events slips from the hands of the statesmen. The difficulty, of course – as Lord Carrington had confirmed to him – lies in knowing how to identify what problems are emerging.

Each year the states of the world spend between them a total of 200,000,000,000,000 US dollars on arms. As a consequence, arms manufacture enjoys the second largest turnover after that of the oil industry. At the time of the Gulf War it was estimated that worldwide there existed

> 70,000 nuclear warheads
> 6,926 long-range rockets
> 400,000 tons of chemical weapons
> 25,500 warplanes
> 740 warships
> 148,000 battle tanks
> 12,100 artillery pieces and
> 21,600,000 hand weapons.

Since then, some nuclear warheads and rockets have been dismantled, and a number of warships – chiefly submarines – decommissioned. These measures have resulted from budget cuts on the part of the great powers; developing countries are continuing to buy as many weapons as they can afford.

Not every individual, and not every nation, has evolved a great deal further than the dog which does not know why it is barking.

GENERAL CONSIDERATIONS

Of the many catchwords which countless people repeat without thinking, the saying that wars achieve nothing is among the most thoughtless. During the twentieth century, war – and war alone – has drastically reshaped the maps, the distribution of population and the balance of power in Europe, the major part of the Near and Middle East and large areas of the Far East. War ended German, Italian and Japanese imperialism, while not a single pacifist has been able to produce a solitary suggestion showing how this could have been achieved without waging war. That inane phrase 'the futility of war', repeated by the empty-headed as though they were trained parrots, is of such breathtaking vacuity that the hand is ashamed to write it, even to condemn.

That war can not only reshape the world, but also save innocent human lives, was proved not least by the Falklands War of 1982. The total defeat of the Argentine forces led to the collapse of that country's military dictatorship and its replacement by democratic government. During six years of military rule, more than 15,000 real or suspected opponents of the Argentinian régime had simply disappeared without trace – a reign of terror which would have continued without Britain's victory.

The atomic bombs dropped on Japan in 1945 similarly saved innumerable human lives. How many years would the war still have continued without these weapons, and how many lives would have been lost on both sides? The Allied Supreme Commander in the Pacific, the US General Douglas MacArthur, estimated that defeating Japan by direct, conventional military means would have cost three million lives.

Anyone else's guess or calculation is equally valid; we can in any case never now prove the point. What is certain is that the lowest possible figure would greatly have exceeded that of the number of victims of the atomic bombs.

Had Saddam Hussein been driven from Iraq when UN troops liberated Kuwait in 1991, one of the benefits would have been an end to his slaughter of the Kurds.

Many things can be achieved through war – good as well as bad.

A much more justified criticism than the 'war solves nothing' nonsense would be that the peace subsequently achieved by war seldom produces a lasting solution of the original problem, tending instead simply to create new constellations of power.

Though only smaller wars were fought in Europe during the 141 years which followed the ending of the Thirty Years' War in 1648, dissatisfaction, rivalries and ambitions brewed up eventually, to the extent that general warfare inevitably erupted in 1789.

Napoleon's final overthrow in 1815 was followed by ninety-nine years without large-scale conflicts, but the last decades before the outbreak of the First World War were filled with an atmosphere of revenge and mistrust, as well as of an arms race of previously unknown proportions.

In other words, the 'cold war' between the Soviet Union and the western democracies, which followed the Second World War, was nothing new. Sudden outbreaks of hostilities erupting apparently out of nothing are admittedly no rarities, but such wars usually affect only the countries immediately involved. Widespread wars engaging great coalitions of states are generally preceded by 'cold wars' of longer or shorter duration. The most important characteristic of these 'cold wars' is that they are easily recognizable as such. It should of course go without saying that it is the statesman's task to find solutions and ways out of difficulties while these are still at the 'cold' stage. Yet so long as just one of the parties in dispute still believes that he can gain some advantage by the use of force, every attempt to resolve differences is likely to remain futile.

For a good hundred years after his death, the great philosopher of war, the Prussian Major-General Carl von Clausewitz (1780-1831), unwittingly exercised a fatal influence in just this respect. With his most-quoted maxim, that *war is nothing but the continuation of state policy using other means*, Clausewitz intended simply a reminder not to lose sight of the political aims of a war. He stressed this point repeatedly, for example with his unequivocal exhortation: *'The political aim is the end, war is the means, and the means should never be considered without the end'*. Despite this unmistakability, the meaning of Clausewitz's admonition is generally overlooked, with the concept of a 'continuation of state policy' incorrectly interpreted to justify naked pursuit of one's own aims.

It was of course not Clausewitz's fault that his still thoroughly valid principles concerning the essential nature of war should be misunderstood and even perverted. It was also no fault of his that he was unable to imagine a time in which, thanks to the invention of weapons of mass destruction, war might promise to become obsolete as a means of state policy. Not only for Clausewitz, but also for the whole of humanity before him, for all of his contemporaries and for the generations immediately following him, war was nothing other than a perfectly normal phenomenon, a natural occurrence, a matter of course in international and even in internal affairs.

It need not surprise us that war much too often produces a situation completely different from that which even the victors have striven to attain. The day-to-day exigencies of the actual waging of war frequently drive his original political objectives from the statesman's mind. As Clausewitz put it, they think of the means without the end – an error which when modern weapons systems are involved can prove suicidal.

Now that weapons of mass destruction mean that a nation entering full-scale war puts its entire population at risk, as well as all of its territory, the possibilities for solving international difficulties with military means have become increasingly problematic. Today's sophisticated weapons systems may promise a speedy (and perhaps less bloody) solution to any crises, but thanks to the same technology they can equally swiftly be intercepted and destroyed. Modern strategic weapons allow neither side much time for negotiation.

One thing is certain: that the assurance of possessing superior arms can all too easily lead to dangerous errors of judgement. In the days when the United States had at its disposal a massive superiority in nuclear weapons for response to any attack by Soviet forces in Europe, experts in Washington deceived themselves into monstrous levels of fantasy. The so-called 'optimum plan' of the US Strategic Air Command foresaw the use of 600 to 700 atomic bombs on Russia in the event of war. On March 15, 1954, representatives of the US Army, Air Force and Navy were assured during a conference at Omaha, Nebraska, that 'in two hours practically all of Russia' would be 'nothing but a smoking, radiating ruin'.

This grotesque overestimate of one's own strength recalls its obverse, the exaggerated fears of the British government before the Second World War, that within twenty-four hours of the start of hostilities all that would remain of London would be a smoking heap of rubble. Acting on this assumption, when war seemed inevitable in August 1939, the authorities ordered a million coffins for the expected victims of the first air raids. The actual total of civilians killed by enemy action in Britain (air raids, cross-Channel shelling, V1 and V2 operations) during almost six years of war was around 60,000.

Fortunately, the American expectation of being able to reduce the Soviet Union to a pile of radiating rubble *in two hours* (!) was never put to the test. Possession of large numbers of nuclear weapons is one thing; delivering these to their targets by bomber (the only means in 1954) quite another. The Soviets already had their first surface-to-air missiles at the time of the rash American calculations; in 1960 they shot down a US spyplane (a U2) during a flight over the Soviet Union, apparently without difficulty.

In wars between industrial nations, technology may indeed become decisive. It may well be that the side possessing superior weaponry, and using it better, will prevail. Industrial nations, however, start with higher expectations and assumptions than less developed peoples. They tend to regard a continuation of fighting as impossible once their sophisticated weapons systems and the facilities of everyday living have been put out of action. Against more primitive enemies, superior weapons technology is effective only to a limited extent. A more primitive people, prepared to absorb all the casualties which the enemy can inflict on him, will be difficult to force into capitulation and will himself prosecute the war with unrestrained ruthlessness. Knowingly or not, he will act in the spirit of another Clausewitz definition: *'War is an act of force, and there are no limits to its use'*.

How much of this use of force can present-day, soft-living industrial peoples endure? If war is to be survived, moral strength must not be absent from a nation's armoury, any more than adequate weapons stocks and other material resources.

Among western peoples, this indispensable moral and psychological preparedness is being eroded by the expectation of being able to conduct an impersonal, 'hands off' war. Reliance on technology alone is totally illusory and can easily lead to the downfall of the more advanced nations. Carnoustie awaits.

As the industrial age progressed, a mode of thinking began to evolve which has since come to dominate man's behaviour: he is looking to science to supply him with an answer to all his problems. In other words, faith in science and technology has largely replaced belief in God. Where once man had automatically asked for intervention from the Almighty to help him out of his troubles, he now expects difficulties to disappear magically thanks to the discovery of some chemist, physicist or biologist. The daily swallowing of countless tranquillizing tablets and other medicinal treatments is evidence of this illusory dependence. People have come to expect from scientists that they provide magical means to abolish all their personal problems without themselves doing a thing. Once they prayed to God; now they go to the dispensing chemist.

In much the same way, present-day governments tend to look to their scientists to supply miracle-working wonder weapons. In itself, this expectation is not new: supposed wonder weapons have been devised and deployed in hope since antiquity, just as the suffering individual has always turned with alacrity to anyone offering miracle cures. The longing for a miraculous solution – whether a medicine, a weapon or an act of God – is a naturally occurring element in the human psyche. It is not necessary to be a golfer to appreciate the power of such wilful self-delusion, as evidenced and exploited in the advertisements for golf clubs and balls. Many millions of pounds are spent annually by amateur players worldwide who are chasing the illusion that a new set of clubs will miraculously transform their scores, that a different ball might fly and roll in greater conformity with their wishes.

In the course of the twentieth century, science has indeed turned many fantasies of fiction writers into everyday reality. From heart transplantation to a landing on the moon, scientists have accomplished what had previously not only been, but also seemed, impossible.

The danger concomitant with these successes is the temptation to rely on further technological progress alone in the search for a solution to mankind's problems. In defence matters, governments throw money into the laps of the scientists and wait for delivery of a weapons system to which the other side has no answer. This attitude leads inevitably to increasing neglect of those personal qualities and virtues which since antiquity have proved indispensable for prevailing in war.

Continuing to ignore these moral factors can bring about one's own downfall faster and more thoroughly than any enemy action. Military potency all too easily seduces its possessor into catastrophic self-delusion. To survive in war requires not just powerful armed forces but also economic strength and plentiful resources in both material supplies and personnel. Equally indispensable sometimes can be support – if only moral – from other countries not themselves engaged in the fighting. This manifested itself with particular clarity during the First World War, when the German and Austrian Empires found themselves practically under siege at the heart of Europe, with few friends. The performance and sacrifices of many first class fighting troops have frequently been undermined due to this very lack of support for their country from neutrals.

Just like the self-assurance of knowing oneself to be better armed than the potential enemy, so success in earlier wars can equally easily lead to a fatal overconfidence. After their sensational victory over the Russian Fleet in 1905, the Japanese as a people felt themselves confirmed in their belief that God was on their side, and were convinced that they must win all future wars. As a consequence of this conviction, though Japan was already deeply involved in a war against China, her leaders did not hesitate in 1941 to declare war on both the British Empire and the United States of America as well. Along with the most populous country on earth, the Japanese selected as enemies the largest empire in world history, covering one-quarter of the earth's surface, and the world's greatest industrial power as well. This unmatched conceit was paid for under the mushroom clouds of Hiroshima and Nagasaki. Here was Carnoustie with a vengeance.

A further effective method of ensuring one's own destruction always comes of as much of a surprise to the suicide himself as to his enemies: it is possible to die of a surfeit of victories. France's power and resources were exhausted in the series of defeats which Napoleon's armies inflicted on her enemies. Imperial Germany depleted her means in beating Tsarist Russia into submission, having then no more reserves of strength to fight off the reinforced assaults of the Allies on the western front. Hitler's *Wehrmacht* (Armed Services) defeated the forces of so many other countries that Germany found herself having to fight on too many diverse and widely spread fronts until she bled to death.

A consequence of the extremely costly sophistication of modern weapons systems is that it is now possible to arm oneself to death in peacetime before even a shot is fired. It is estimated that military expenditure of the Soviet Union during the 'cold war' amounted to some twenty-five per cent of gross national product (GNP), compared with some six per cent by the British and Americans. The result was total collapse of the bankrupt state.

It was not military necessity which drove the Soviet Union into self-destruction, but the delusions of her political leaders, who for decades allowed their prejudices and obsessions to detach them from reality.

Students of military matters are repeatedly compelled to occupy their thoughts with the unwelcome subject of politicians and their follies. It is, after all, not the nation as a whole which produces situations creating wars, nor is it military men – except in the rarest of cases, such as that of the Japanese General Staff in the 1920s and 1930s. Whatever forces may be at the root of international resentments, it is the actions and failures of a nation's leaders which convert these into war.

What frequently happens is that the statesman's motivating idea, whatever it may be, is distorted into obsession by wilful blindness, vanity and, frequently, sheer ignorance. Whether an economic theory, a religious dogma or simply the concept of the nation itself, the idea becomes more important to him than the individual.

Particularly despicable is the politicians' practice of blaming anything and anyone else for the results of their actions or inaction, of being 'not available' for comment when trouble crops up, or of despatching a junior colleague into the firing line. How can military men possibly retain any respect for governments and ministers who behave like this and yet expect to give instructions to the armed forces? Readiness to accept responsibility for the consequences of one's actions is, among other things, what makes a real man out of what is otherwise, until proven to be a man, merely a human designated medically as 'male'.

The question of true gender characteristics invites consideration of that proposition much touted among earlier generations that 'if women ruled the world, there wouldn't be any more wars'. Since we have seen a number of women in power, few people will have difficulty in recalling some who have shown themselves no better or more humane than their male counterparts. We see them similarly deluding themselves into over-dramatization, confusing a know-it-all attitude with capability and, which is so much worse in a woman, mistaking wilful heartlessness for strength. The myth that our search for peace might be aided by a general feminization of politics is easily dispelled.

All character defects are serious; when the individual has in his or her hands the power to determine the course of others' lives, faults become dangers-in-waiting. Citizens in dictatorships must endure without redress; in democracies we suffer from the limitations of the pool of those from whom our leaders are drawn. We are not permitted to nominate for parliament persons of proven character, ability and worth, but are compelled to select the lesser evil from among those proposing themselves. It is a system far worse than Hobson's choice, since at Hobson's stable at least there were some first class horses available which one would draw sooner or later.

It would be convenient to attribute politicians' errors to normal human fallibility, no different from the weaknesses to which we are all prone. Such tolerance is made more difficult by the way in which parliamentarians frequently forfeit both our sympathy and our respect through contemptuous dismissal of very real concerns among the people and the persistence which they parade their conviction that in all things they know better than the rest of us. This attitude only reveals a level of conceit in inverse proportion to ability. An honourable exception here, as in so many other matters, is Switzerland, where a true democracy implements the clearly expressed will of the people on vital issues.

Of course, to castigate politicians as a breed would be, like all generalizations, both silly and unfair. Even in an age when entering parliament has become a matter of a personal career with profits rather than of service to the nation, there may still be some decent people engaged in politics, and occasionally perhaps even some able ones. Nonetheless, it is imperative always to maintain an ultra-critical watch on those in whose hands might lie the responsibility either for bringing about war, or at least of failing to prevent it. Their errors are always paid for with the blood of a young soldiery innocently trusting in the judgement of its leaders. Today the bill is met by the civilian population as well.

Discovering the limitations of one's personal abilities is perhaps the first essential for soundness in the adult personality. If this insight has even developed at all, the act of entering politics appears to dislocate it.

Wars are often decided at an early stage, with the loser continuing to fight bitterly – and senselessly – causing pointless deaths on a massive scale. The First World War provides an example. With the French 'miracle on the Marne' (halting the German advance at the river), this war was actually already decided in September 1914. This should have been clear to everyone by the end of that year at the latest, by which time the entire front had frozen into a sterile line of trenches stretching from the Channel to the Swiss frontier. Any effective participation in the war on Germany's part was dependent on her ability to force France into rapid capitulation by encircling Paris, in order then to be able to turn all her forces against the Russian giant. With the end of German forward movement on the Marne, well to the east of Paris, the game was already over. In view of the massive superiority of Allied forces in East and West, the outcome of any further fighting was effectively preprogrammed. Had diplomatic peace feelers been extended around Christmas 1914, and not fallen on deaf ears, not only would all the belligerents have been spared the horrendous losses of the next four years, but any peace then concluded would certainly not have included the punitive clauses of the later Versailles Treaty – and the peoples of Europe would then also have been spared the Second World War.

Yet whose national pride, already swelling as is natural in war, would have allowed him to recognize after this first Marne battle that the die was already cast? So long as it remained possible to persuade oneself that there was still something to be gained, with the nation having already made considerable efforts and having casualties to mourn, the feelings which had been aroused on both sides inevitably ruled out any chance of a cease-fire. To have seized the moment to make peace without any further suffering would in 1914 have required the keenest insight alongside coolest objectivity – probably, too, it would have needed the hindsight advantage of considerable distance from the events, such as we now enjoy. Even at a much later stage of the war, it would have been extremely difficult to persuade anyone of the pointlessness of continuing the fight. It is a fact that lost causes usually induce a tenacious continuation of the struggle, even when, as was not the case in 1914, the hopelessness of the fight is recognized. Reluctance to abandon an undertaking once begun is part of human nature. Without this determined spirit, man would have achieved a great deal less than he has – yet thanks to this same spirit he also inflicts a great deal of unnecessary suffering on himself.

What Germany lost on the Marne was her forward momentum. No amount of tenacity and sacrifice could help her regain it. Even in the war of movement conducted by Hitler's forces, his operations were to fail through this same loss of dynamic impetus. Hitler neglected to destroy the British Expeditionary Force during the fall of France, allowing survivors to escape to Britain and regain their strength; he lost his momentum in Russia through dividing his forces between separate objectives; and in Africa he was brought to a halt on a narrow front near the coast (at El Alamein), from which the Eighth Army was to drive him back at record speed.

Nowadays, the nation at home enjoys practically immediate vicarious participation in battlefield events, thanks to modern electronic reporting media. Television pictures play a massive part in forming public opinion. More than any other factor, the impressions which they gain from television determine the attitudes of a people, in belligerent as well as in neutral countries. As unpleasant as this is in a free society, it is consequently more important than ever for governments to control war reporting, in order to avoid any negative effects on operations and on public support for these.

Dictatorships, though not given to considering public opinion and in any case less likely to experience the emergence of any 'anti-war' movements, exercise strict control over reporting as a matter of course. They enjoy a further advantage over democracies in being able to indulge in long-term planning – something undertaken less keenly in states anticipating repeated changes of government due to swings in the inclinations of an electorate.

It is as if Clausewitz had dictatorships in mind when he wrote:

'In so dangerous a matter as war, the errors arising from good-naturedness are the worst. The one who uses force ruthlessly will prevail, if his opponent fails to do likewise'.

This is a lesson which even the democracies have had to learn, discovering the necessity of repaying like with like.

The moral perceptions of what is permissible in war are continually changing, not only from era to era, but even in the course of a single conflict. During the First World War, the British at first declined to read the encoded radio traffic of Germany's diplomatic service. Listening in to military signals and decoding these was regarded as a legitimate act of war; diplomatic messages on the other hand were considered sacrosanct. This is how considerately one was prepared to treat the civilian enemy in 1914. Little more than a quarter of a century later, Britain introduced unrestrained bombing of German cities.

The Americans, too, were once inhibited by chivalrous scruples. In 1929 they disbanded that very department of their intelligence service which listened in to the encoded traffic of other nations, among them, naturally, Japan and Germany. Their reason: 'A gentleman does not read another's letters'. It was only 16 years later that these same Americans dropped two atomic bombs on Japanese cities. This is how rapidly the ethics of warfare changed during the twentieth century.

Each act of war, in generating its specific dynamics, creates imperatives of its own.

TRENDS

In antiquity it was customary to massacre a defeated people. Early wars were a straightforward matter of kill or be killed.

By the time of Frederick the Great of Prussia (1740-86), customs and morals had meanwhile advanced so far that Frederick saw no reason for the nation to notice when his armies were at war. Whereas life for the ordinary citizen in those days was unquestionably harder than our own lives 200 years later, warfare in Frederick's day must be acknowledged as having been particularly civilized. It was not then regarded as disgraceful to break off hostilities without having achieved a definitive conclusion. Armies were sent into the field, manoeuvred in search of a good position until encountering the enemy, and fought, unless compelled to do otherwise, only when they considered their situation favourable. Soldiers in those days generally fought on only two or three days in a year. If war were found to be leading to no concrete outcome, peace negotiations would be started without loss of face. Armies could be withdrawn from the field without this being received as a national catastrophe.

In crass and suicidal contrast, twentieth century peoples and statesmen seem to have felt it essential to fight out a war until the enemy was either completely destroyed or battered into total capitulation. Such an attitude no longer has any place in a world armed with nuclear weapons.

It should be remembered that war was once an affair of kings and other rulers; generally speaking, it is only since the eighteenth century that it has become a matter for entire nations. National states are a relatively modern institution, and national feelings a comparatively recent evolution.

Just like the kings, princes and local potentates of earlier times, these national states once waged war on their neighbours for possession of just small strips of territory or even only of a strategically placed town. The scale has altered. Expectations are greater; nothing less than utter humiliation of one's opponent is regarded now as sufficient.

It is probably the emergence of a continuous front which has led to this modern hardening of political attitudes and the growth of a mentality which sees in war nothing less than a fight for survival or death of the entire nation.

In the First World War, once the destructive effects of the new defensive firepower had brought all forward movement to a halt, uninterrupted static lines of battle developed on both eastern and western fronts. This meant that, unlike his ancestors who had fought on only two or three days in the year, the ordinary soldier was now in action *every* day, and frequently at night as well. The repeated attempts of both sides at breaking through to end the stalemate resulted in battles of attrition. In turn this led to mobilization of the whole nation to supply and support the fighting troops. So-called 'total war' had arrived.

Every belligerent nation now had fresh casualties to mourn each day, unlike the occasional losses of earlier generations. Continually suffering losses leads inevitably to hatred and intransigence. As long as engagement is uninterrupted, there is little willingness to discuss peace. Warfare round the clock means that only being overrun or compelled to recognize the hopelessness of further resistance can bring about an end. This became apparent in the Second World War just as in the First, even though the later conflict was essentially a war of movement without static front lines.

This characteristic of modern warfare, continuous physical engagement on the ground, may perhaps be moderated by the use of long-range, strategic weapons, but continuity of engagement in time, if not on the ground, will still remain the dominant feature. Future belligerent nations, too, will have an uninterrupted list of casualties to mourn. Engagement with the enemy will still take place continuously, in some place or other, in some form or other, even if 'only' via intercontinental ballistic missiles or laser weapons fired from space.

The feelings of hatred engendered by total war have brought about a return to the barbarities of antiquity, a reversion to conduct which would have horrified our immediate forebears. Whenever ideology or religion is involved, warfare is particularly cruel and ruthless. This was especially the case in the Thirty Years' War (1618-48), yet despite the religious fanaticism with which it had been fought, even this horrific war was concluded with a peace distinguished by its chivalry. The Treaty of Westphalia neither apportioned blame for the war, nor dictated reparations. On the contrary, the peace terms guaranteed *'permanent amnesty for all actions which have been committed in the course of hostilities from the beginning, at any place and in any fashion, by either side'*. Both fighting men and civilian officials were guaranteed that they would suffer *'no disadvantage or prosecution'* and that *'no punishment or penalty'* would be demanded *'under any pretext'*. This waiving of punitive treatment of former enemies in no way meant *carte blanche* for any future aggressors. Article One of the treaty expressly decreed that the peace must be *'a Christian, general and permanent'* one, and that punishment awaited anyone who might break it.

This was certainly an example of just that farsighted understanding so tragically missing in the statesmen of the twentieth century. Hatred and thirst for revenge dictated after the First World War that all the blame would be heaped onto the side which had been battered into asking for a cease-fire, and that this alleged sole guilt would be used as an excuse to impose peace terms of such a punitive nature that they made the Second World War inevitable. As even the Allied Supreme Commander, the French Marshal Ferdinand Foch, so prophetically exclaimed when he saw the terms of the Versailles Treaty in 1919: *'That is no peace. That is an armistice for twenty years'*.

Germany had, after all, been the last to mobilize in 1914, doing so only after both Russia and France had mobilized against her. Mistreating a defeated enemy as Germany was mistreated at Versailles must prove self-defeating. Fear of encountering the same sort of vengeful attitude on the part of one's enemies as the Allies displayed at Versailles can only deter any belligerent from extending peace feelers. Any such expectation must engender the bitterest resistance, lengthening the horrors of modern war in an unnecessary fashion. One should not just, as Clausewitz defined it, place the enemy *'in a situation which is worse than the sacrifice which one is demanding from him'*. One must also always offer him a tempting way out of hostilities.

The horrendous human losses in the wars of the twentieth century were not a consequence of any increased inclination to war. The annual average of two fresh wars each year had been maintained for centuries. To start with the post-Napoleonic period, the total killed in wars between 1820 and 1863 amounted to some two millions. Around 4,500,000 were killed in the wars fought between 1864 and 1907. From 1908 to 1950, there were altogether some forty millions killed in war. This rise in the numbers of casualties during periods of comparable length, despite no increase in the numbers of wars, emphasizes only the increase in destructive firepower, along with the emergence of continuous fronts.

Interestingly, the very next period of similar duration, from 1951 to 1994, saw the total of war dead sink for the first time, from some forty millions to around twenty millions. This trend, too, was due to the increase in weapons potency – in this case, though, it was thanks to their deterrent effect. One hundred or so wars were fought during those forty-odd years, yet the existence of nuclear weapons kept the leading powers from going to war against one another. It is noteworthy that wars are now being unleashed only by states not under threat from nuclear weapons.

Blind to the indisputable lessons inherent in these figures, the leading nations, currently in possession of significant nuclear arsenals, agreed at the United Nations in May 2000 to abandon these.

Civilian populations, in so far as they were within the reach of enemy forces, were direct victims of war throughout antiquity, as well as during the Middle Ages. It was once a matter of course that an enemy population should be regarded and treated as both victim and booty. In time, such practices were abandoned, very probably through realization that what one might do to one's defeated enemy today could be visited on oneself tomorrow. Whatever the reasons, more restrained treatment of the enemy's civil population came to be the custom, even if non-combatants have at no time been completely immune from atrocities. Gradually, wars became matters almost exclusively for armies and fleets, until France's revolutionary leaders undertook a deliberate attempt at mobilizing the entire nation for their wars.

France fought a continuous succession of wars against her neighbours for several decades at the end of the eighteenth and the beginning of the nineteenth centuries. It seems not to have mattered to Frenchmen whether they fought for Louis XVI, for the revolutionary First Republic or later for the Empire of Napoleon. They died for what they perceived to be the interests of their nation at the time, any internal differences being immaterial.

It was new weapons, the greater mobility of armed forces and above all air power, which ensured that civilians in the twentieth century would be drawn totally into war.

The rapidly rising proportion of civilian casualties illustrates the extent to which modern warfare has become a matter for everyone, just as it was in antiquity. Only every twentieth victim of the First World War was a civilian; in the Second World War, almost as many civilians died as servicemen. The Korean War caused five times as many deaths among the civilian population as among the fighting troops; in Vietnam the civilian dead outnumbered the military fallen by a factor of eleven to one.

In one respect, the course of the First World War already represented something of a return to the warfare of the Middle Ages, in that Central Europe was turned into the scene of a massive siege. Just as had happened in earlier ages to the inhabitants of an encircled town, the German and Austrian Empires were starved into requesting an armistice, ground down by years of merciless Allied blockade. These events inevitably spread the waging of war to encompass the entire civilian population.

The concept of strategic air warfare arose from the wish to avoid the mutual slaughter of armies numbering millions. It culminated in the construction and use of the first atomic bombs, thus finally and irrevocably shifting the centre of gravity of warfare from the soldier to the civilian.

The leaders of any state armed with nuclear weapons are given much cause for reflection once their potential opponent is similarly armed. It is not a preponderance of these warheads which is decisive, but the ability to deliver them with certainty to their targets. Even the capacity to deliver an overpowering surprise attack, a 'first strike', does not guarantee success. What matters is the ability to hit back with a 'second strike' despite losses sustained. Possession of this ability gives even a state which is itself in the process of disintegration the means to take its assailant down with it.

Alongside the certainty of being able to inflict a first strike successfully, it is no less essential to be sure of parrying the enemy's retaliatory second strike. Since, however, the history of arms development is filled with examples of supposed 'wonder weapons' which in action have failed to achieve their intended effects, it would be foolish of any government or military high command to take for granted anything other than the possibility that everything can still go disastrously wrong.

Despite superior weapons technology, both the Americans in Vietnam and the Russians in Afghanistan were defeated in the end by a determined people who by comparison were primitively armed. In each case, a faith ingrained throughout the population – in the one case ideological, in the other religious – was to prove decisive. In Afghanistan, the resoluteness of the Islamic fighters against the Soviet invaders was based on the conviction that death in a holy war would bring immediate entry into paradise. It is difficult to imagine more convincing proof of the necessity for taking account of psychological factors, both during and before a war, than these humiliations for the two great powers.

Americans and Russians had both tried to keep their own battlefield losses low by going over to a fast war of movement by means of helicopters. The attempt failed in each case.

In the words of Mao Zedong, the guerrilla fighter moves like a fish in water, undetectable among the ordinary population. In both the Vietnam and the Afghanistan wars, guerrillas succeeded in making the regular troops opposing them long for an end to the fighting and for the earliest possible return home. Americans and Russians alike soon had no other thought than the question how long the fighting would continue. An army whose soldiers count the days in this fashion is already beaten.

Among other things, partisan warfare enables a state to wage war against its enemies by proxy. The Soviet Union financed North Vietnam's war against the United States to the extent of 13 million US dollars daily, while Afghan's Islamic fighters against the Soviets were supported by the Americans. Each power attempted in this way to frustrate the efforts of its opponent on the world stage to extend his own power or sphere of influence. An increase in vicarious partisan warfare is to be expected during the coming century from just such motives, whenever it is too risky to act directly against a nuclear-armed rival.

It must be assumed that the generally disregarded rules of war laid down in the Hague Convention of 1907 will in future be ignored completely by partisans. The convention prescribes four basic laws for irregular warfare: partisans must be organized under the command of leaders who take responsibility for their actions; they must wear uniform or a badge of some kind (frequently an armband) recognizable at 300 metres (rifle-fire range); they must carry their weapons openly; and must obey all other rules of war (no killing of unarmed prisoners who have surrendered, and so on). Disregard of any one of these laws means forfeiture of the partisan's own protection under the same rules.

Just as tempting for the great powers as the possibility of waging war by proxy is the recent dream of so-called 'hands off' warfare. To some extent, the technology already exists for such remotely-controlled offensive actions – but the idea of being able to wage a completely impersonal war solely by push-button while sitting in an impregnable bunker is just the sort of notion all too easily leading to fatal over-confidence, to yet another repeat of the fundamental error of exaggerated and unfounded hopes.

One thing is unlike to change: the recurrent tendency of politicians to waste and to make a nonsense of the self-sacrifices of their young, trusting soldiery, if not during the war, then at least afterwards, through weak-kneed submission and short-sighted decisions round the table.

It is not so much the dictator's proverbial delusions of grandeur which we have to fear; these usually manifest themselves in good time and cannot catch us by surprise. Much more dangerous, because insidious, are the ordinary politician's delusions of adequacy.

POPULAR SELF-DECEPTION:
ALLIANCES, NEUTRALITY, PACIFISM

Those new constellations and power structures which tend to emerge from any war frequently result in the same foreign policy phenomenon: the enemy from the last war becomes an ally in the next.

It was France which for centuries was the repeated violator of European peace. Fresh coalitions of other European powers had continually to be formed to contain France and her ambitions. Not until recent times did Germany replace France as Europe's troublemaker. Most countries then turned against Germany, with the ancient French enemy welcomed willingly as an alliance partner against this new threat. After 1945, the Soviet Union emerged as the greatest danger to peace, so that the next great coalition had to be formed against Moscow. Inevitably, *both* sides now tried to win the former German villain as a military ally. With the collapse of the Soviet Union, China might well appear on stage as the next disturber of the peace. In such an eventuality, no one need be surprised if Russia should be greeted with open arms as a partner in a military alliance against the Chinese.

Unless they are concluded for purposes of joint aggression, alliances formed during peacetime have a dual intent: they are meant to preserve peace by deterring a potential enemy; and, should deterrence fail, they guarantee the contracting nations that at least they have already secured allies for the fighting. A great deal of value is placed on the idea of 'collective security', and it cannot be denied that the existence of mutual assistance pacts have indeed proved their capacity to deter attempts at aggression or to dampen down expansionist dreams. A *sine qua non* here, of course, is that for deterrence to be at all effective the determination and resolve of the alliance partners must be unmistakable. NATO is an excellent example of this.

Despite such self-evident successes as that of NATO, the disadvantage of alliances concluded in peacetime must not be overlooked: they tie the hands of the treaty partners, leaving these no room for manoeuvre as the international situation changes.

In an age when wars are no longer fought far from home, risking only the loss of an expedition force, when wars instead mean jeopardizing the continued existence of the entire nation, alliance commitments can prove self-defeating rather than advantageous. All the same, no nation finding itself at war should be alone.

Hitler's appalling choice of allies, Italy and Japan, made matters even worse for Germany. When British forces began to drive Italian invaders out of Egypt, Mussolini asked Hitler for the assistance of a *Panzer* division. This became the *Afrika Korps*, the total loss of which helped to bleed Germany dry. The Italians were thrown out of Greece and became hard-pressed in Albania. Once again, Mussolini asked for German aid. Hitler sent twenty-five divisions with 1,200 tanks and 780 aircraft via Yugoslavia into Greece. Besides the further loss of strength, this action meant postponing for five weeks Hitler's scheduled invasion of Russia. The delay was to prove fatal to the Russian campaign, as winter set in exceptionally early and halted the German advance right at the outskirts of Moscow. In observance of his Tokyo alliance, Hitler next declared war on the USA when Japan attacked America – whereas Japan did nothing to help in Germany's war on Russia. This was a one-sided and suicidal alliance, if ever there was one. Bringing in the industrial and military might of the USA against Germany ensured destruction of the Reich.

Hitler had no decent allies, and did nothing to deserve any. One of his most significant errors was that he never made clear what Germany's war aims actually were. Why had the German *Reich* gone to war, and for what was it fighting? The German people no doubt had their own ideas, but what did the rest of Europe know of Germany's objectives? What convincing arguments could or did Hitler produce to persuade Germany's neighbours to enter the struggle voluntarily on her side?

Instead of a German announcement of certain specific war aims, there was only vague talk of a creating a 'new order' in Europe. What form this new order was to take was never explained – the crassest failure of propaganda by a régime which was normally a master in that field. What sort of society the newly ordered states would receive at the hands of a victorious Germany was something which the peoples of the largely occupied European mainland were never to learn. They had to fear the worst: namely, that the hardships of German occupation would become a permanent state. It was understandable that under these circumstances they preferred not to throw their weight behind the Axis, particularly since the prospect of a German defeat at least promised a return to the independence of pre-war days. Why anyone should hope for a German victory, let alone want to fight at Germany's side, escaped those very peoples of Europe who from Hitler's point of view should have been won over for the Axis cause.

In stark contrast to this negative picture of Hitler's war aims, the Western powers from the outset left no room for doubt about the outcome for which they were fighting: liberation of the occupied countries and abolition of the National Socialist régime. The occupied peoples were able to hope for an Allied victory which would bring them a future of peace and freedom. Admittedly, this expectation was doomed to be disappointed in those countries which were assigned in 1945 to the Soviet sphere of influence. All the same, the Allies' positive approach welded their coalition more firmly together, while denying the Axis the support of many neutral countries.

As it happened, the picture of a firm union of the Allies during the Second World War, with its repeated propagandistic representation of the four or five flags of the nations fighting together (Britain, France, the USA, the USSR and sometimes China as well) was in several respects misleading. Not only was the coalition of the capitalist powers and their mortal enemy the Soviet Union anything but sincere; in addition, the Americans were already intriguing against their European friends while the war was still in progress. At the 'Big Three' conferences, Roosevelt took the first opportunity to go behind Churchill's back in order to work out with Stalin the undermining of Britain's pre-eminence in the world.

Roosevelt was anxious not to have a British Empire as a rival in the post-war world, and looked for an alliance with Stalin to work towards this end. France, too, in Roosevelt's eyes, would have to lose her overseas colonies. The President suggested to Stalin that French Indochina (which included Vietnam) should first be placed under international administration for forty or fifty years, and then given independence. From this, Stalin knew while the war against Hitler was still raging that he would have no opposition to fear from the Americans in undertaking any subversive actions in colonies of the European powers. With Washington's consent he would be able to establish and support communist movements all round the globe.

In all this, Roosevelt overlooked the simple – and, one would have thought, very obvious – fact that Stalin's concept of the post-war world differed very severely from his own. Unwittingly, the terminally ill US President gave the signal to start the Vietnam War, as well as other communist adventures, as early as the Yalta conference. These disasters had to be dealt with by some of his successors in office, and paid for with the blood of young soldiers.

It will always be power – that is, military potency – which proves decisive in international affairs. There can never be reliance on groups of nations or on international organizations in which each country enjoys an equal voice. The Greeks of antiquity learned this lesson very early on. Every member in the coalition of states formed to resist the expansionist efforts of Athens had the same voting rights, yet when the military situation was at its worst, it was the strongest and most capable state, Sparta, which had to assume leadership. Without the Spartans' decisive actions, all other Greeks would have fallen victim to the Athenians' imperialist ambitions, instead of which the power of Athens was finally broken (in 404 BC) after twenty-seven years of bitter fighting.

The lessons contained in this ancient experience remain equally valid for NATO, the European Union and the United Nations. In the UN General Assembly in particular, the equal voting rights of developing countries can have disastrous effects for the advanced nations.

Recognizing the dangers of tying one's hands, the Swedes have sought to avoid these perils by entering no military alliances. Anyone attempting to emulate Sweden's course will undergo the Carnoustie trauma if he believes that neutrality of this kind will allow wars to pass by his country, leaving it untouched. The dream of neutrality is fulfilled only for nations which do not stand in a belligerent's path, and which in addition are themselves armed to a level of credible deterrence.

In no sense is Sweden an unarmed country, any more than is Switzerland. Sweden, though belonging to no military block, has more warplanes in service than Germany, a full member of NATO. She is proportionately more strongly armed than the UK, having *per capita* nine times as many battle tanks and a Home Guard which can be ready for action in two hours.

Unlike Sweden, which was able to preserve her neutrality in both world wars, the Kingdom of the Netherlands was in 1939 of geographic-strategic importance. The significance of their country's geographical location for both sides seems, inexplicably, to have escaped Dutch leaders. Since the Netherlands had succeeded in remaining neutral throughout the First World War, and had actually been a supplier of Fokker aircraft to the German forces, the Dutch appear to have assumed in 1939 that once again they could stand aside from the firing. The Low Countries, where airfields could be created very quickly almost everywhere, would have provided an ideal network of bases for the RAF to attack Germany's vital industrial Ruhr region, just across the border.

Hitler prevented any such development by himself occupying the Netherlands in 1940. With an invasion of Russia imminent, the same considerations played a part in Hitler's decision to occupy Greece in response to Mussolini's plea. Stalin had kindly supplied three-eighths of Germany's oil in 1940, including high-octane aviation spirit for the *Luftwaffe*'s role in the Battle of Britain. The remainder of Germany's fuel came from Romania. Once he invaded Russia and ceased to receive fuel supplies from her, Hitler would be totally dependent on his Romanian sources. Operating from bases in Greece, British bombers would have been able to cripple the

Romanian oilfields. Hitler's Balkan invasion prevented this. There were no demands which Hitler had made or was about to make on Greece, and no matters of dispute existed between the two nations.

The same applied to relations between the Netherlands and Germany. Neither the Dutch nor the Greeks had, however, realized that their geographical situation must inevitably draw them into hostilities. They also appear to have overlooked the simple fact that neutrality is not a role which a nation can choose for itself; others decide whether one is to remain neutral. A country not invaded for its own sake might still be occupied by one side, simply to deny it to the other.

In general, it can be useful in any conflict for one or two states to remain neutral, if only to act as channels of communication between belligerents (peace feelers, exchange of wounded and so on). Yet with the great mobility of present-day armed forces, no government can assume that it will be able to maintain neutrality.

The desire of those wishing to remain neutral, to remain untouched by other people's wars, may be perfectly understandable, but comes nonetheless into the category of wishful thinking. In future, 'pacifism' is doomed to come under the same heading. It is impossible to foresee any possibilities in future wars of offering the civilian greater protection from enemy fire than soldiers will enjoy. Modern warfare is for everybody. Those pacifists who, like the Scottish National Party, argue for an abandonment of the present level of their own country's defence efforts in favour of 'neutrality on the Swiss model' would be in for an almighty shock were this policy actually to be implemented. Switzerland, with a population less than one eighth that of Britain, has nearly twice as many battle tanks as the UK and almost two and a half times the number of trained soldiers available for instant mobilization. For Scotland to have armed forces on the same scale as the Swiss would mean, in the same proportion to the population, maintaining fifteen times as many battle tanks and twelve times as many warplanes as at present.

Alongside paying the increased taxation which would be necessary to finance this intensified level of armaments, the Scots

72

male would also need to adapt to a quite different lifestyle were the Swiss pattern to be followed. This would mean, first, conscription at age 20 for basic training, with refresher training as a reservist annually thereafter until age 32. From age 33 to 42, he would need to undergo training for the militia. He would be required to fire a prescribed minimum number of rounds annually at a rifle range and to maintain a certain standard of marksmanship. His complete infantryman's equipment would be kept at home, ready for instant mobilization.

Even more arrogant than the presumptive self-delusion of the 'pacifist', that he will be spared the hardships of war, is his automatic assumption that he and he alone cherishes humane values and conducts himself nobly. There is little to be admired in standing aside when fellow-humans need help. Though they are probably incapable of seeing things this way, what pacifists and disarmers are suggesting is a surrender to lawlessness and unrestrained violence. Being disarmed increases the difficulty of ending matters quickly when trouble erupts, and it certainly deters no one.

The issue is not really a complicated one. Disarmers and pacifists have yet to suggest how our being disarmed would have deterred anyone from the invasions, occupations and annexations which have filled the twentieth century, or how such disarmament would have helped to liberate any of those occupied countries and their people. The answer, of course, is simple: our noble pacifists and disarmers would simply have left the hapless victims to their fate.

Being prepared to fight, and being seen to be prepared, at least gives one some sort of a chance of deterring another's aggression. At worst, it puts one in a position to try to end trouble quickly.

Armed forces reflect the civilian societies from which they are drawn, with all their virtues and, equally, with all of their weaknesses. Whether an army in action distinguishes itself by its sense of duty and willingness to self-sacrifice, or is disgraced through individual selfishness, indiscipline and lack of stamina, are questions already resolved before war starts.

In past ages, a study of the arts of war was regarded as the noblest calling for a man. Understandably, a more experienced mankind is now no longer satisfied with such aspirations. In particular, the natural idealism of youth demands more humane activities than going to war. Yet can there be any act greater in spirit than oneself accepting the hardships, suffering and sacrifices of war in order to defend or to liberate others attacked by a third party? It is only the war of aggression waged out of greed which is reprehensible.

In war, many people may sink to a level of conduct which is frankly bestial. Unquestionably, though, war also brings out the very finest in mankind – acts of heroism, endurance and self-sacrifice unimaginable in our comfortable everyday lives. The true nobility of man finds no finer expression than in the sheer selflessness displayed on the battlefield.

Doubtless those calling themselves 'pacifists' would be surprised to discover that fundamentally all people are pacifists at heart – and none more so than those having direct experience of warfare, which most proclaimed and active 'pacifists' do not.

Despite man's powerful instinct to wage war, it is an undeniable fact that his basic nature also includes a natural disinclination to kill his fellows. Other creatures do not generally kill members of their own species; *homo sapiens* is one of the few to do this at all. Yet a remarkable number of soldiers display a reluctance to fire directly at an enemy even in the heat of battle, when it is undeniably a matter of kill or be killed. Researches conducted immediately after battles have uncovered the astonishing fact that on average only one infantryman in seven had used his rifle at all; even in particularly tight corners the figure has rarely been higher than one in four. Evaluation and release of these study results have astounded no one more than the very soldiers concerned. Every man failing to fire had assumed that he had been the only one to have indulged in pretence; he had kept his head down and gone through the motions. By contrast, weapons which need a team to operate are fired without pause; no one wants his own reluctance to be seen by his comrades.

The inhibitions lying at the roots of these completely unexpected results allow a little hope. Unfortunately, only a little.

THERE IS WAR, AND THERE IS WAR

Hitler failed in the end because he had not considered seriously before invading Poland who might be drawn into the fight; did not ask himself what sort of warfare his enemies might wage; consequently did not anticipate any weak points on the other side; as a result did not think out what arms he would need to exploit his enemies' weaknesses; and so failed to build the German *Wehrmacht* into the sort of forces necessary to ensure victory.

Like Russia, Germany was and is a continental land-based power. The thinking of Germany's political and military leaders, the expectations of her people, her entire national psyche have all been shaped naturally by German origins, history, traditions and archetypes, with the result that war is perceived fundamentally as a struggle *on land* around all the frontiers of German territory. The promising debut of the Imperial Navy's submarine arm during the First World War did nothing to alter the basic German view of war as a series of land battles.

Even the *Luftwaffe* was created chiefly as 'flying artillery' to serve the fighting troops on land as a spearhead of attack. Initially, the *Luftwaffe* did indeed carry out this task brilliantly, but remained integrated into the concept of land warfare, expected to mount attacks only against targets within a limited radius ahead of the ground troops' advance. Despite these conceptual limitations, the *Luftwaffe* more than once played a strategically decisive role (for example in the battles for Norway and Crete), but its tasks were always seen as subordinate to Army needs.

War for Germany, even a war on multiple fronts, should have been fundamentally simple, though admittedly not easy. Germany's fighting fronts were served by internal lines. In the event of an intensified attack by the enemy at any particular point, there were no insurmountable obstacles to redirecting defensive forces and supplies to the areas of crisis. If increased enemy pressure should be felt at several points, or even overall, defence could be stiffened by shortening the fronts, bringing the further advantage of shrinking lines of supply and communication. Hitler, though, resisted all shortening of the front lines on principle. His refusal to withdraw forces increased the difficulty of defending the *Reich*.

Similarly, the Soviet Union faced straightforward tasks both in resisting German invasion and in going over to the offensive. The Soviets, too, had only internal lines of supply and communication to secure, and could concentrate all their efforts on the sole task of advancing over ground.

Because of the nature of the warfare which Germans and Russians felt obliged to conduct, neither of these two opponents had created a strategic air force. It is admittedly questionable, in view of the hinterland space available to Russia, how far strategic air war against her would have weakened her industrial and defence potential. It is certain that any such assault would have strengthened rather than broken the fighting spirit of the Russian people.

Russia's massed tank armies, supported by an exclusively tactical air force, were optimally equipped for westward thrusts. For their part, Germany's armed forces were well capable of defending the *Reich* against her immediate neighbours, and even of defeating these, but more were involved than just immediate neighbours.

The British, and later the Americans as well, were compelled to wage another kind of war altogether.

In the absence of a joint land frontier with their enemies, further participation in the war by the British depended, once France had fallen, on their being able to ship across the seas and oceans huge numbers of troops and immense quantities of *matériel*. This capability demanded mastery of the seas, which in turn became increasingly dependent on control of the air. This last became clear during the battles for Norway in April 1940, when warships and supply vessels on both sides fell victim to the bombs of enemy aircraft. Without a single drop of oil either in home soil or in British waters, waging war at all was for Britain totally contingent on oil imports. Not a single British wheel could turn, not an aircraft take off, no factory go to work, without the arrival of tanker vessels at home ports. A complete German sea blockade would very quickly have compelled London to negotiate a peace.

Yet Hitler ignored the urgent peacetime plea by Admiral Dönitz to build a fleet of 300 U-boats for the event of war with Britain. Such a fleet would have been fully adequate to put Britain out of the war. Even had Britain refused to make peace, a U-boat fleet as envisaged by Dönitz would still have remained necessary to prevent the transport of American munitions and troops across the Atlantic and to rule out all possibility of an Allied invasion of the Continent. Germany would have remained undisputed master of the European land mass.

As it was, the German Navy did not put in a full appearance even during the evacuation from Dunkirk, when the opportunity was presented both to destroy the basis of the British Army and to inflict serious losses on the Royal Navy's complement of vessels.

Hitler's basic error was in failing to realize that his provocative conduct of foreign policy would inevitably land him with ultimatums and declarations of war. He plunged from one undertaking to another, without any overall concept. Incredibly, Hitler failed to appreciate the implications of Britain's guarantee to Poland and simply did not reckon with a British declaration of war. His remaining errors – failure to create either an adequate U-boat fleet or a strategic bomber force – were a consequence not so much of this late miscalculation as of an earlier absence of far-sightedness and long-term planning.

Well before embarking on his challenging foreign policy, Hitler had built up his *Wehrmacht* according to *his own* ideas of warfare, not – as he should have – in accordance with the demands of the kind of war which his *enemies* would force on him. The *Wehrmacht* was created for rapid, decisive forward thrusts across the boundaries of the *Reich*. *Blitzkrieg* (lightning war) was tailor-made for the geographical situation of a nation which might find itself at war with neighbours on all sides. It was the warfare of the German, a central European, *Reich*.

From the outset, *Blitzkrieg* was never an option for the British and Americans. Where there is no common land frontier with prospective enemies, rapidly moving tank armies, supported by dive-bombers, are not a great deal of use. After the fall of France,

Britain's only means of continuing the fight were to cut off Germany from all imports by sea and to destroy her industries and lines of supply from the air.

This is a completely different form of war, shifting the centre of gravity from the fighting front to the homeland, in order to undermine the armies in the field. This type of warfare can be countered only by using the same means, which Hitler failed to do effectively because he had allowed his enemies too great a lead. Even his V-weapons arrived too late to enable him to catch up.

Warfare is in any case always conducted on numerous levels, the battlefield encounter for physical mastery reflecting the outcome of simultaneous struggles in the fields of technology, the economy, ideology, psychology, subversion and espionage.

There are only two ways to end a war. The cheaper, and classic, way is to persuade the enemy of the uselessness of further resistance. By differing means, this was achieved with both Italy and Japan. The other, far more costly, method is physically to destroy the enemy's fighting capability. This is what happened to Germany.

The Second World War was not *one* war, but several wars simultaneously. Each of the belligerents fought *his* individual type of war, the sort conforming to his own strategic situation. It was just this which for some proved to be the critical error leading to their defeat. They should have waged the kind of war which was directed at *the enemy's* situation, not one suited to their own.

TWO KINDS OF ERROR – TWO WORLD WARS

The actions which triggered off both world wars are well enough known: the assassination of the heir to the Austrian throne by a Serbian-backed Bosnian nationalist in 1914, and the invasion by German troops in 1939 of what was at the time Polish territory.

On the other hand, few people understand either the exact sequence of events leading in each case to the outbreak of hostilities, or the actual motives lying behind these.

Very few wars break out of their own accord. In most cases, an atmosphere of hostility has already arisen years beforehand among the later belligerents. A 'cold war' precedes the hot one.

Long before the murder at Sarajevo, fatal emotions had been at work. These ranged from France's thirst for revenge over her defeat by Prussia in 1870 to Austria's fearfulness that her empire might break up completely, thanks to Russia's interfering hand. Russia was driven by a sense of mission to unite all the Slav peoples in one pan-Slav movement – naturally under Russian leadership.

Between 1891 and 1899, the French strengthened their links with Russia, with whom they formulated concrete plans for joint military action. As early as the beginning of 1894 – fully twenty years before war came – France and Russia had concluded specific details of mobilization and deployment of their forces not only against Germany, but against Austria-Hungary as well. In 1899, the French and Russian governments agreed to use their military power not just in emergency, for defensive purposes, but also with the objective of maintaining the balance of power in Europe. This was another cynical instance of the Clausewitzian 'politics using other means' – and *not* on the part of the Germans.

Germany herself had worried France by making colonial claims (Morocco), and had caused concern to Britain with the ambitious expansion of her navy. Certainly the Kaiser was, and is still widely, believed to have wanted war and to have prepared feverishly for it.

It is likely to come as a surprise to learn that at the outbreak of war in August 1914, Germany's output of artillery pieces was running at a level of just fifteen per month. A figure of one new gun every two days scarcely suggests any headlong rush into aggression. Nor does the German level of conscription, which was of course practised in peacetime in most countries of Continental Europe. Whereas pre-First World War Germany called up a bare fifty per cent of all those eligible for military service, France, on the other hand, conscripted more than eighty per cent.

For several weeks after the Sarajevo assassination, the Germans undertook no steps whatever to prepare for going to war. On the contrary, Germany's Foreign Minister, Count von Bethmann-Hollweg, urged Vienna to negotiate with Russia to bring about a peaceful resolution of the confrontation with Serbia.

While both London and Berlin were trying to secure a diplomatic solution, the French had already assured Russia of their military support. The route to war was set – not just in a metaphorical, but in the literal sense as well. Russia mobilized her 2,500,000 soldiers, setting them off in trains towards Germany and Austria.

In view of Germany's efforts to act as mediator, the Tsar attempted to reverse the mobilization against Germany, downgrading the general mobilization already started into a partial mobilization directed against Austria alone. It is at this point that the researcher discovers to his horror that the suffering of millions was caused by the purported impossibility of switching over the points on the railway lines which were leading directly into war. The Tsar was told that practical reasons prevented a reversal of the troop transport timetable. An operation already under way, involving two and a half million men, was simply too vast for reversal.

The *de facto* course of events, as opposed to the impression created by newspaper cartoons of the day, indicates no particular determination to go to war on Germany's part, and certainly no sole guilt. Quite apparent, on the contrary, is French determination to use any excuse to go to war against Germany, ignoring even the rights and wrongs of the situation *vis-à-vis* Serbia's complicity in the Austrian assassination. To this was added Russia's ambition to break up Austria-Hungary at all costs. The French pledge of military assistance to Russia amounted to a premature declaration of war on Germany. It was not Germany which was first to mobilize against her enemies, but the other way round.

The Versailles Treaty of 1919 burdened Germany with sole responsibility for the outbreak of the First World War. This charge was unsupported by the evidence, though many Germans, in their justifiable pride at Germany's achievements since 1870, had thoughtlessly laid the foundation before 1914 for an accusation that Germany had been looking for an opportunity to start a war. Their aggressive swaggering had been the German sin; it was foolish, but was not a crime.

Serbia was to emerge from the First World War as the only real winner – that same Serbia which by backing the Sarajevo assassination was the actual guilty party in launching a war which brought about the collapse of four empires: the German, Austrian, Russian and Turkish. Unlike the great powers, Serbia herself suffered only minimal losses, while all her ambitions were fulfilled: the Austrian Empire was dismantled and a Greater Serbia with access to the sea was created – the later Yugoslavia.

The price exacted from Germany for her miscalculation (bringing Britain into the war by violating Belgian neutrality) was the vindictive Treaty of Versailles. The lesson to be learned is obvious: restrict conflicts to the specific objectives – which must be attainable – inherent in the *casus belli*.

This same error, of losing sight of the actual objective and making more enemies than was necessary, was committed twenty-five years later by Adolf Hitler. All the same, he did do rather better than his predecessors, coming alarmingly close to achieving victory.

The First World War broke out because the great powers of those days were over-hasty in mobilizing and in issuing ultimatums. Before they could look round, their own premature actions had brought about a military confrontation which could not be stopped.

The conflict would have been worth avoiding. Of the sixty-five million men mobilized worldwide between 1914 and 1918, ten million were killed and twenty million wounded, a third of these being permanently crippled. The fighting created ten million refugees, five million war widows and nine million war orphans, while more than three and a half million people simply disappeared. The belligerents' financial expenditure on the fighting would at the prices of those days have provided every family in Britain, Canada, Australia, the USA, France, Belgium, Germany and Russia with a house, fully furnished, on a one-acre site; would have built a library and a university in every town with more than 200,000 inhabitants in all of those countries; would in addition have left enough for a fund to yield an income from interest for the salaries of 125,000 nurses and the same number of teachers; and over and above this would have still been sufficient to purchase every already existing piece of property in both France and Belgium. These calculations do not even include the additional costs of war such as the interest on loans and the pensions paid to widows and the disabled.

These figures make abundantly clear what an incredible bargain we enjoy in modern nuclear deterrence. They also help us to understand those fears which led Neville Chamberlain to tell an audience in 1938 that *'in war, whichever side may call itself the victor, there are no winners, but all are losers'*.

Though Germany had unjustly been assigned sole guilt for the First World War at Versailles, even Britain's then Prime Minister, David Lloyd George, admitted later that *'we all slipped into the war'*. Acknowledging this earlier error, Britain and France were anxious during the 1930s not to repeat it. Only too aware that not enough time had been allowed for diplomatic negotiations in 1914, they avoided adopting a threatening stance towards Germany, despite Hitler's disturbing foreign policy activities.

This attitude, too, proved to be a mistake. The lack of any reaction by the western powers only encouraged Hitler to further risky adventures. The first time, too pugnacious; the second, too indulgent. Both ways turned out in the end to be mistaken.

THE WAR NO ONE WANTED

It has become an axiom that each war is fought with the methods of the war immediately preceding it. It would be more accurate to observe that states at war tend to continue tried and proven tactics and strategies, while the winner is likely to be the one who first recognizes any new possibilities, masters these and applies them successfully.

Battlefield tactics from the Second World War may in general have long since lost their value as patterns for future operations. All the same, this was a war which provides several useful lessons from different perspectives: for example as a war of ideology, as a war of technology and also as a war of escalation. The student is helped immeasurably by the fact that more records are available for the Second World War than for any other encounter in history.

More than anything else, the Second World War presents an excellent example of the psychological elements in conflict. These psychological factors are usually overlooked not only by the general public but equally by the statesman and the academic researcher. Numerical comparisons of armed strength have become an everyday fashion, a measure used by peace-loving nations – and almost certainly by calculating national leaders, too – as a basis for speculation about the behaviour of a potential enemy, the likelihood of war and its outcome. Rational standards of reasoning are applied in making these assessments, despite the fact that both history and the present day provide us with countless instances of wars started and fought out from motives which are completely *ir*rational. The disastrous role of human emotions in the origins and conduct of the Second World War are there for all to see, yet it tends to remain submerged under the opaque mass of information about those years.

Just like the Imperial German Government of 1914, Hitler too appears to have believed that he could localize the initial conflict. He was incapable of understanding that his own behaviour, forcing through one piece of territorial aggrandizement after another, undermined confidence in his word and unleashed understandable fears among the other peoples of Europe. No one could be sure where, when or even whether he would stop.

Curiously, the propaganda of the National Socialist régime itself was probably more responsible than anything else for the growth of this fear, presenting as it did a picture of a nation armed to the teeth, solidly behind its leaders and prepared for anything. The image was deceptive. In the first place, Hitler himself was far from being certain of where he was heading, feeling his way forward step by step like a blind man with a stick. In the second place, the *Wehrmacht* possessed nothing like the strength which its propagandists like to portray in newsreel films.

Were it not for the fact that Hitler did indeed later prove to be rather wolf-like, one would be tempted to describe the Third Reich on the eve of the Second World War as something of a sheep in wolf's clothing. The result of the fearsome image presented was that a potential weapon for exerting successful pressure was over-applied to the extent of scoring an own goal, calling into being an anti-German alliance motivated by fear. A properly calculating Hitler could have spared Germany the declarations of war made by Britain and France, if, for example, he had pursued a different timetable for his actions. His fundamental error lay in making his first move the occupation of the Czech republic, rather than the invasion of Poland. If Hitler had moved against Poland first, without having previously destroyed Czechoslovakia, there would almost certainly never have been any British-French ultimatums and declarations of war.

Perhaps, though, Hitler annexed Bohemia and Moravia from the Czechs out of military considerations, feeling it essential to secure his southern flank before fighting the Poles. If this were the case, then it is evidence that Hitler had already decided in the spring of 1939, when he moved into the Czech state, that he was going to invade Poland. This in turn would mean that all Germany's later negotiations with Warsaw were sheer hypocrisy.

Hitler's action against the Czechs, in defiance of his solemnly given word at Munich, made the British feel that they had been cheated. They had bent over backwards to meet the man halfway, and he had broken his word. This feeling ran through the entire nation. Anyone allowing himself to be duped by a swindler becomes greatly annoyed not only at the one who has tricked him; he also feels very angry with himself for having been so foolish as to be taken in. He becomes absolutely determined never to fall for such a trick again. The victim's anger at his deceiver turns rapidly into determination to have his revenge at the very next opportunity.

Hitler aroused hostility which caused his later appeals for peace to fall on deaf ears. In essence, everything happened at the wrong time. Looking back, it is easy to recognize that the western powers should have acted with armed force in March 1936, when Hitler sent troops into the demilitarized Rhineland in defiance of the Versailles ban. Decisive action then would have prevented the later, larger war. It has emerged since 1945 that Hitler himself had expected the British and French to intervene in the Rhineland; he had merely been testing our resolution.

Yet would any step into war by Britain and France have been justified in 1936? Did the remilitarization of the Rhineland present an adequate *casus belli*? It is certain that any such action on our part would have been condemned by large sections of the public at home, as well as by other countries, as premature and over-hasty reaction. No democratic government can lead its country into war without the more or less complete support of its people.

While it was undeniable that the entry of German troops into the Rhineland was a clear breach of peace treaty conditions, those conditions themselves were of very dubious character. After all, the Rhineland was internal German territory. It is certain that the British and French peoples would not have given their governments united support in taking military action against Germany on such doubtful grounds. It is equally clear that British and French armed forces were not strong enough in 1936 to have prevailed against the small but brilliantly trained and well-equipped *Wehrmacht*.

By the time that British and French forces had been strengthened and Hitler's repeatedly broken word had allowed the psychological climate in Britain and France to mature into readiness to fight, it was already too late. Neither physical preparedness nor moral willingness for war was there until Hitler for his part could no longer deterred from a military course. This is the whole tragedy. While there was still a chance to prevent catastrophe, no one was prepared, either physically or morally, to do anything. Before people were ready to act, the opportunity had already been missed.

THE WAR NO ONE COULD STOP

Conducting affairs of state in peacetime is something like driving a motor car through city traffic. It is frequently necessary to turn aside from one's chosen course, to avoid obstructions and unexpected hazards lying in wait along the preferred route.

Once war has broken out, driving becomes increasingly more difficult. In certain circumstances, steering can break down altogether. Events develop a momentum of their own, turning a motoring trip into a runaway big dipper ride offering no means of either steering or braking.

Wars which cost fewer lives than the belligerents had been prepared to accept at the outset are historical rarities. One such, at least for the Allies, was the Gulf War of 1991 – though the exceptionally low losses in this case are at least partly explained by the fact that the Allies contented themselves with doing only half a job. Declining the opportunity to sweep away Saddam Hussein and his régime kept Allied losses below the expected level. A job left half-done, however, scarcely affords a satisfactory example.

To later generations, the causes of almost every war appear at the best inadequate, if not completely incomprehensible. With the objectivity of the bystander, a later observer examines the overt matters in dispute before the outbreak of hostilities (perhaps some question of frontiers and sovereignty) and shakes his head in bewilderment that what appear to him secondary difficulties should have led apparently unthinkingly into self-destructive war. All such objective analyses are inevitably founded on consideration only of tangible, measurable factors. The psychological driving forces producing war are usually completely overlooked. Yet it is psychological motivations which provide the impetus to war, and which therefore demand to be understood.

Wars do not originate in the sphere of rational thought, but in the realms of human emotions. Even when it is calculation which actually determines the step into war, perhaps to take advantage of a favourable situation, the motivation behind the decision is always an emotion, whether greed, hurt pride, stubbornness, lust for revenge, outrage over an injustice or straightforward hatred. Anyone seriously interested in preserving peace needs to understand the evolution of feelings like these, which make people more or less blind to rationality. He must not overlook the fact that hatred, too, has its roots, and that these need to be taken into consideration. However insubstantial and unjustified those roots may be, they are convincing enough for the one who feels the hatred.

While aroused emotions can bring about a war, the same effect quickly begins to work in reverse: the conflict itself raises the emotional temperature in its turn, frequently to the extent that methods of waging war go off the rails. Hitler's attempted destruction of the Jews provides the worst possible example of this.

Adolf Hitler undoubtedly possessed great gifts, but at the same time his personality was a very narrow one. His incapacity to imagine the effects of his actions on other people was literally to prove fatal for millions. Hitler conducted foreign policy in a fashion which can be described only as primitive. Thanks to his behaviour, Hitler managed to accomplish the astonishing trick of inducing bitter resistance in others even when he was making justified claims. If he had started out deliberately to make sworn enemies of neighbouring peoples, he could scarcely have chosen a more effective way of setting about this than the way he did behave. To dismiss Hitler's aim of destroying European Jewry as evidence that he 'must have been mad' is valueless. Any such simplistic evasion brings us no nearer to understanding that particular atrocity. Yet is this not a political subject, rather than a military one?

Let us first try to discover what considerations could have led to such an act. Hitler appears from his youth onward to have blamed the Jewish people for all that was bad in the world. His speeches and comments during the war years confirm that he held 'international Jewry' – whatever that may be – responsible for the escalation of a regional dispute (his campaign against Poland) into a world war and for the fact that Germany found herself facing a world full of enemies. Hitler seems to have imagined sinister Jewish figures in Paris, London and Washington, who had egged on their governments into war against Germany.

However absurd such a conspiracy theory may seem to us, what is essential about it is that Hitler himself believed in it unshakeably. Even in his final testament, dictated immediately before he committed suicide, Hitler repeats and stresses this view.

Twenty years earlier, referring to the First World War, Hitler had commented in his book *Mein Kampf*:

'If twelve or fifteen thousand of these Hebrew corrupters of the nation had been held under poison gas at the start of the war, in a way such as hundreds of thousands of our best German workers of all classes and occupations had to endure, the sacrifice of millions at the front would not have been in vain.'

Hitler, who had himself been temporarily blinded in a British poison gas attack in 1918, used equally unequivocal language in his *Reichstag* speech of January 30, 1939:

'If international financial Jewry, both in Europe and outside, should succeed in plunging the nations into a new world war, then the outcome will not be the bolshevization of the world and with it the triumph of Jewry, but rather the destruction of the Jewish race in Europe.'

During the war, Henriette von Schirach, wife of the former leader of the Hitler Youth, protested to Hitler about the deportation of Jews from occupied Holland. Hitler's response was the angry contention that while ten thousand soldiers were being killed every day, there was a lack of balance. Hitler appears to have been arguing that so long as the German people were suffering casualties, the Jews should also have theirs.

Willi Schneider, a member of Hitler's bodyguard, is another witness to this sort of remark. Schneider confirms having heard Hitler say that the Jews too would have to suffer, so long as ten thousand German soldiers were dying every day in an attempt to defend European culture.

Of themselves, these few quotations are no proof of anything. They are only indications, yet taken together they appear to throw some light on the way that Hitler's attitude evolved. He seems to have believed that the Jewish people were out to destroy Germany, and had to be punished for this. If this was indeed Hitler's motivation, then the attempted destruction of Europe's Jews indeed belongs as an episode in the history of war, as a most grotesque example of the side-effects which wars can sometimes produce.

The driving forces producing such excesses are fear and hatred, the one being born out of the other.

The Second World War presents a classic example of a war of escalation, not just in a geographical sense with expanding theatres of operations and the entry of ever more states, but also because the conduct of warfare itself was intensified, culminating in death camps and the atomic bomb. Increasing bitterness developed not least because both sides were fighting for their ideological obsessions, as well as for life or death of the nation. It was not just National Socialism and communism which were waging a battle to the death. Americans and British, too, became increasingly motivated by equally powerful convictions, as the title of General Dwight Eisenhower's book, *Crusade in Europe*, confirms.

All the same, the Second World War did not develop into a struggle for national survival solely because of the ideology involved. The impression that the war was one to decide life or death of the nation itself was reinforced by the fact that every citizen of the belligerent nations, except for those of the USA and of the Soviet Union east of Moscow, was liable to be bombed from the air. Technical progress had enabled and brought about total war, producing an excess of hatred on all sides.

The Allies were motivated by a single unifying aim: complete destruction of Nazi Germany. The conspirators against Hitler, chiefly *Wehrmacht* officers, overlooked the fact that the Allies wanted the total defeat of Germany itself as a nation; that they held the military equally guilty with Hitler and would never have negotiated a peace with German generals; that they wanted to make the German people realize that this time they had been utterly defeated; and that they wanted to prevent any possibility of a new 'stab-in-the-back' legend such as had arisen in Germany after 1918.

The Allies had justified the First World War to their own peoples by means of an anti-German atrocity propaganda which was largely invention. After the Second World War, revelation of the German death camps made it appear that this time the Germans had gone out of their way to make the Allied cause a just one.

AERIAL WARFARE

Battlefield tactics tend to lag behind weapons development. Possibilities for the most effectual use of new weapons are generally not understood at first. Battlefield success goes to the side which is first to recognize new opportunities and to apply them effectively. A typical example is the advent of the tank during the First World War. This invention offered a way out of the stagnation of trench warfare. It had been constructed for just such a purpose, yet there was no grasp of how to deploy the tank for maximum effect. The tank's potential was squandered initially by its being deployed in small numbers to support conventional infantry attacks.

It was left to later thinkers – Fuller, Liddell Hart, de Gaulle, Guderian – to make possible a less bloody war of movement through the creation of independent armoured formations.

Yet simultaneously with this all too familiar backwardness in tactics evolution, a 180-degree reversal in the customary relationship between technology and tactics was taking place in quite another field. Whereas previously technical progress had always been more rapid than the development of either tactics or overall strategy, with the invention of the aeroplane the imagination of many military minds raced for once far ahead of the actual physical possibilities offered by the new machines.

When the Frenchman Louis Blériot flew across the Channel to England in 1909, every Briton abruptly became aware that the sea and the Royal Navy no longer necessarily guaranteed secure defence of his island home. Alarmed by this realization, and recognizing that a large-scale European war was likely, Hugh (later Lord) Trenchard, a 40-years-old cavalry officer and veteran of the Boer war, had himself taught to fly.

During the First World War, Trenchard commanded the Army's Royal Flying Corps, whose aircraft he deployed as far as possible in attacking roles in support of land offensives. He saw aircraft basically as instruments of attack, the sky being, as he saw it, *'too big to be defended'*. This was unquestionably an accurate viewpoint, given the level of technology of the day.

Where Trenchard had instantly grasped the offensive possibilities of air power, the Germans demonstrated no such rapid insight. German airmen thought and flew chiefly defensively, guarding their own front and venturing over Allied lines only for reconnaissance purposes.

This neglect was particularly noticeable at Verdun, where it cost Germany a possible chance of turning the war to her advantage. French soldiers fighting around Verdun had to be supplied via a single road, thirty-six miles long, over which an endless column of no fewer than 6,000 lorries went back and forth every day, carrying ammunition, food and all the other battlefield necessities. This solitary supply route would have been easy to destroy from the air, yet during all the long months of the Verdun battles no German aircraft attacked even a single French vehicle along the entire length of the vital artery. Germany's Verdun offensive was an ingenious strategic initiative aimed at bleeding France's forces to death, yet her General Staff overlooked the very tool, right there to hand, which would have enabled it to succeed. This was an only-to-be-expected example of the customary failure to recognize new possibilities.

By contrast, Trenchard, meanwhile Chief of the Air Staff, brought about in 1918 the marriage of the Royal Flying Corps with the Royal Naval Air Service, to create the Royal Air Force. This new service, the world's first independent air force, was conceived by Trenchard from the beginning expressly as a strategic bomber force – a role authorized and indeed favoured by Britain's leaders.

German bombing raids on British cities and towns, which had begun as early as December 1914, had left a deep impression on the entire population. Not only great centres such as London, Glasgow, Newcastle, Leeds, Manchester, Liverpool and Birmingham had been attacked, but also smaller towns such as Folkestone and Margate. Paris had been bombed at the beginning of the war, and it was Germany's policy to carry the war directly to the British people as well. The coastal towns of Scarborough, Hartlepool and Whitby had been bombarded from naval ships, and air raids were another logical dimension to this form of warfare.

The main targets of British bombing raids on Germany during the First World War were munitions factories and steelworks, though here too innocent civilians became victims: 126 children and twenty-six women were killed in one British raid. The French also bombed targets in the German homeland, such as a poison gas factory at Ludwigshafen. These first beginnings of strategic air warfare had no effect on the overall course of the war. All the same, Trenchard had a vision of being able to decide future wars solely by the use of strategic air power, eliminating the need for bloody land battles. Trenchard's concept found many adherents at home, and some abroad. The American General William Mitchell, himself an airman, concurred, arguing for years without success the case for an American bomber force after the British pattern. General Giulio Douhet, commanding Italy's airmen, propagated the same vision in a book published in 1921.

All this had been anticipated by Frederick William Lanchester, an Englishman who had worked out the physical laws governing heavier-than-air flight even before the first powered aeroplane had been constructed. Lanchester produced the earliest mathematical thesis on the theoretical principles of aerodynamics in 1897, only one year after having built Britain's first motor car. All his aerodynamics calculations and predictions were to be proved correct. A man with more than four hundred patented innovations to his name, Lanchester was a member of the Advisory Committee on Aeronautics. He also made a detailed study of battlefield attrition, producing a mathematical guide (the *n-square* law) for calculating the effect of wartime losses on each side's fighting capacity. Always ahead of his time, Lanchester published a book in 1916, *Aircraft in Warfare*, urging the creation of massed warplane fleets.

Between the two world wars, the British and (to a lesser extent) the American air forces were built up as bomber arms. Curiously, in doing so the RAF made the same error which the Germans had committed during the First World War. Thanks to the overall concept of a strategic role for air power, the necessity of attacking armour, artillery and other battlefield objectives from the air was overlooked. As a consequence, the RAF started the Second World War without adequate tactical aircraft formations, paying the price for this omission during the 1940 Battle of France. The lesson was learned. Four years later, the RAF returned to France with a new generation of aircraft, whose air-to-ground rockets were now largely to dictate events on the battlefield.

Between 1939 and 1945, the RAF and USAF dropped a combined total of 2,770,540 tons of bombs on targets in Europe. German civilian casualties of the raids have been estimated at one million, with 3.6 million German homes destroyed. Strategic air warfare had drawn civilian populations back into war to an extent not seen in Europe for 300 years. The paradox was that the whole idea of strategic bombing had been to prevent repetition of the horrendous human losses of the First World War.

The high rate of civilian casualties was due primarily to the difficulty for bomber formations of striking only military or industrial targets. Out of 1,006 RAF bombers which set out for Bremen on June 25, 1942, only eighty managed even to find the city of Bremen – and this was no isolated case. It was repeatedly found that not even the target town could be located with certainty, much less the targets of military importance within that town. Long before the Bremen disaster, it had already become clear that it was not possible to hit a factory only, without incidentally damaging the adjacent residential areas. The RAF had for example decided in January 1941 to attack Germany's centres of fuel production. In these raids, only three per cent of bombs dropped fell within a five-mile radius of their intended targets.

A switch to area bombardment was the inevitable consequence: so-called carpet bombing with as many bombs as possible on a given area, accepting civilian casualties as inevitable but also putting out of action at the same time – almost incidentally – targets vital to the enemy's war effort, such as factories and railways. The centres of industrial production specified as targets were inevitably residential cities and towns, of which forty were categorized as being absolutely vital to German war production and a further fifty as of great importance.

As is well known, an additional object of the bombing was an attempt to break the fighting spirit of the German people. Air Marshal Arthur Harris, the head of Bomber Command, was not one of those who believed that German morale could be broken by aerial bombardment; he assumed, correctly, that the war could be won only by destroying Germany's military potential.

It had been calculated in Britain that it would take fifteen months to render one third of the German population homeless. Each ton of bombs dropped was expected to deprive up to 200 hundred workers of their homes and to kill seventy-two people – the so-called 'Barcelona ratio', derived from bombing results during the Spanish Civil War. Had such effects indeed been achieved, the war would have been over very much sooner. By 1945, British and American bombing had been enough, according to the formula behind these original expectations, to have wiped out the entire eighty millions population of the Greater German Reich two and a half times over!

In order for bombers to strike targets of military importance, the tough, comprehensive and effective German *Flak* defences left no alternative to 'laying' carpets of bombs from a great height. Despite persistent assaults from the air, total German industrial production fell in 1943 by only nine per cent, while the output of munitions was increased.

At the opening of the bomber offensive, Churchill had advised on the radio: *'The German civilian population can easily avoid all hardships. They need only to leave the cities, to give up their work'*.

The Japanese people followed this advice, 8.5 millions taking to the safety of open fields. Despite these precautions, a single raid on Tokyo by 334 B-29 Superfortresses killed 120,000, destroying seventeen square miles and burning out forty per cent of the capital. This raid constituted the most destructive six hours in the entire history of warfare. Yet even with devastation on such a scale the militarily important targets could not always be found. In another raid on Tokyo, most bombs fell into the waters of the harbour; in a third, 200 US bombers failed to hit a single factory. During a six-months air offensive against Japan, between October 1944 and April 1945, twice as many civilians were killed as Japanese servicemen during three and a half years of intensive warfare against the United States and the British Empire. Sixty-five Japanese cities were bombed, the economy collapsed, severe food shortages set in. The railway network was crippled, electricity supplies were frequently interrupted and food rations were reduced to 1,500 calories daily. The morale of Japan's civilian population was severely shaken and the mass evacuation of cities initiated.

In contrast, neither Germany's infrastructure nor her fighting spirit collapsed, though the surrender with little fighting of many German towns and cities, and the absence of the expected resistance by *Werewolf* units, was perhaps largely due to the psychological effects of years of bombing. If this was indeed the case, then the strategic air war, though not rendering land battles unnecessary, nonetheless saved Allied, as well as German, lives. Many servicemen were indeed saved by the fact that the air war tied down 1.5 million Germans for air defence of the *Reich* (fighter units, *Flak*, radar, communications and so on), who would otherwise have been used at the fighting front.

The British of all people should have realized from their own experiences of 1940/41 that aerial bombing cannot be relied on to make a determined nation give up the fight, and that it is more likely to weld a community more firmly together. London alone was bombed for no fewer than seventy-six nights in succession during 1940, without collapse of the people's morale. Just as a hunter must load his gun with ammunition suited to his particular prey (no rabbit cartridges against elephants, and vice versa), so too psychological warfare must be adapted to the precise mentality and psyche of the specific enemy. A strategic air offensive aimed at breaking the enemy's will to fight would have been better directed at the Italian rather than at the German people.

Yet there had been other, quite different reasons for Britain's air assault on Germany, above all the psychological need after the fall of France to feel that one was carrying on some sort of offensive warfare against Germany. Such a feeling was an absolute prerequisite for maintaining the fighting morale of the British people – and for the time being there were no other means available for carrying the fight to Germany than by aerial bombing.

Thanks to the Allies' air offensive, the fighting power of the *Wehrmacht* was eventually undermined. Munitions and fuel no longer reached Germany's forward troops, so that the fronts gradually collapsed. Yet this all took much longer than had been envisaged at the outset.

Curiously, *Blitzkrieg*, of which *tactical* aerial bombing was a fundamental constituent, brought about that drastic reduction in casualties initially expected on the Allied side of its *strategic* use. By startling contrast with the fruitless carnage of 1914-18, the six-weeks campaign which subdued France and the Low Countries in 1940 cost Germany only 27,000 dead. Poland had been overrun with only 17,000 military dead on both sides, including the losses of Hitler's Russian allies, who invaded Poland from the East. This low-cost warfare was possible only so long as one side alone had mastered and employed *Blitzkrieg*. The Allies were not slow in learning to do likewise, and the casualty rates then rose.

Land warfare did not become superfluous, not even through the massive strategic onslaught which cost the loss of no fewer than 15,516 Allied heavy bombers. It was only the use of atomic weapons against Japan which finally eliminated the need for confrontation on land, made an invasion of the Japanese homeland unnecessary, shortened the war, saved countless lives and promised to realize the original dream of the fathers of strategic air warfare.

In Vietnam, American aircraft dropped a greater total bombload than they had throughout the Second World War, without being able to defeat the enemy on the ground. It was left to the Gulf War of 1991 to provide final confirmation that air power has greater potential to decide the outcome of war than land battles. The success of Allied air forces admittedly did not render land fighting superfluous in the Gulf, though ground battles were reduced to a minimum thanks to destruction from the air of critical Iraqi positions, troop concentrations and supplies.

It was always risky to attempt to fight a war with the same methods as in the preceding conflict. It will be particularly dangerous to expect an equally easy victory in any future war as in the Gulf, when Allied airmen were able to put Iraqi forces out of action very quickly. Another time, the enemy is likely to be rather better armed and led.

Iraqi targets were attacked with considerable effect in 1991 by cruise missiles fired from US B-52 bombers in flight. In 1992, the US Strategic Air Command was wound up, and all American nuclear weapons placed under a new Strategic Command, though if necessary a B-52 can be converted within fifteen minutes to carry atomic bombs.

The role of air forces has returned to tactical areas: reconnaissance; intervention in battlefield actions including destruction of tanks and artillery; elimination of enemy air power; attacks behind the front lines on the enemy's reserves and supplies; cutting his communications, and so on.

The era of strategic bombing was only a brief one, occupying barely seventy years. Its death was proclaimed by the Americans' fruitless bombing of North Vietnam. All the same, in 1982 an RAF Vulcan heavy bomber established a new long-range world record for a bombing raid, making a return flight of 8,000 miles to drop twenty-one bombs on Port Stanley airfield in the Falklands, making the facility useless to the Argentinian occupation forces. This raid, strictly speaking a tactical action as part of the preparations for a land offensive, represented the swansong of an aircraft designed in the early 1950s exclusively for strategic use, carrying atomic bombs.

As a strategic weapon, the bomber has been replaced by the long-range rocket, whose deployment against the enemy's industry, infrastructure and civilian population promises the same war-winning effects once expected of the aeroplane. It is a promise which will be fulfilled only so long as nuclear warheads remain available. The pinch of salt to be taken with pledges to abandon these weapons can be poured from the cellar of the following considerations:

Agreements on levels of arms serve diverse purposes. Sometimes they are concluded in order to slow down the other side until it can be overtaken; sometimes in good faith to try to limit the danger in an arms race; sometimes for propagandistic purposes, to reassure the public either at home or abroad; sometimes in order to ease the burden on the state purse; sometimes to assist in the re-election of a democratic leader or government; sometimes to anaesthetize a prospective victim with the illusion of security and receding danger.

Disarmament can serve all these purposes; one purpose it can never fulfil, and that is to prevent aggression. This can be achieved only by an unmistakably adequate level of arms with an equally unequivocal determination to defend oneself.

Campaigners for nuclear disarmament should ask themselves honestly whether they would have opposed use of the first atomic bombs, had these been ready three years earlier than they were: not in August 1945 but in August 1942, when the extent of both German and Japanese conquests was at its fullest.

Response to this hypothetical question reveals a great deal about the individual.

DREAMS AND NIGHTMARES:
LESSONS FROM THE GULF WAR

A mere six days after Kuwait had achieved full independence with the ending of the British protectorate in June 1961, Iraq's then military dictator, General Kassem, announced that Kuwait was part of Iraq. Such a claim lacks any foundation, either historically or juridically. Kuwait had been founded by Arab nomads, and already existed as a British protectorate before the state of Iraq was created out of the old Ottoman Empire. What attracted the Iraqis about Kuwait were the gigantic oil reserves discovered in the tiny neighbouring sheikdom by an Anglo-American company in 1938. Kassem's posture in 1961 triggered off a call for help, in response to which British troops landed in Kuwait to oppose any possible Iraqi invasion. After Kassem had been deposed in a 1963 *coup*, his successor recognized Kuwait's independence.

Economically exhausted after eight years of war against Iran, and coveting Kuwait's giant oil resources for her own recovery, Iraq occupied her small neighbour in 1990, in defiance of her own earlier assurances. Iraq, meanwhile possessing the world's fourth largest army with one million men under arms, was fifty times as strongly armed as Kuwait. When a military coalition, including some Arab countries, was formed to free Kuwait, Baghdad devised a new form of propaganda in an attempt to dissuade western states from military action. Press conferences were staged in early 1991 in an effort to spread fear of the ecological consequences of battle. Scientists were produced before television cameras to describe in graphic detail the environmental damage which military action against Iraq's forces would entail. This represented an attempt to exploit fears fashionable among western populations, in the hope of inciting popular movements to dissuade their governments from attempting to liberate the occupied dwarf state. This effort to disarm the other fellow morally from within failed miserably. Nonetheless, it presents an interesting example of propagandistic inventiveness. A democracy can scarcely ever go to war without at least the tacit consent of the majority, and in this television age the opportunities for influencing public opinion are greater than ever before. Men of the Saddam Hussein type know only too well how to exploit other people's fears; this is the very breath of their life, since their own existence depends on the terror which they themselves inspire at home. Waging modern warfare demands complete understanding of these propaganda dangers, alongside mastery of one's own means of retaining public support. A peace-loving government which fails to recognize the importance of these matters will quickly be doomed when the balloon goes up. The most sophisticated weapons systems will be of little use if the people's will to act has already been undermined. Not all nations have the same tolerance to pain, and the enemy will never be slow to exploit understandable reluctance to sustain casualties. The Chinese, Japanese and Russians for example can fight on after suffering losses which would force European peoples to their knees.

At the other extreme, US troops were withdrawn from Lebanon in 1984 once they had sustained 223 dead. Such events do not go unnoticed by calculating men such as Saddam Hussein, who can use them to estimate with reasonable accuracy the threshold of pain of the American people and their leaders. This threshold does not of course remain at any constant level; it varies according to the importance and vulnerability of the national interests which need to be defended or are perceived to be under threat.

In his estimate of American unwillingness to suffer losses, Saddam Hussein was not so far wide of the mark. He may not have been able to deter action to liberate Kuwait, but the American leaders of the military coalition broke off hostilities without exploiting the opportunity to sweep away the régime in Baghdad. Saddam came away unscathed from his gamble, without being called to account for his breach of the international peace. The outcome in the Gulf suggested the case of an armed burglar, breaking into a house to steal valuables; killing the owner, raping the owner's wife and destroying a great deal of property; opening fire when the police arrive; setting the house on fire when he is finally chased out – and then not being pursued by the police but allowed to run safely home, killing a few policeman as he goes. No arrest, no charges; the whole incident is forgotten in a welter of satisfaction at the fact that the burglar is no longer in the other fellow's house, and even of gratitude that more policemen had not been killed during the burglar's escape.

It is scarcely necessary to mention that a society which acted this way towards criminals would be doomed to a never-ending crime wave. Why, then, for goodness' sake, does the family of nations allow international assault and robbery to go unpunished and indeed to flourish?

The fact is that there exists no established mechanism by means of which a state exercising violence can be either stopped in its tracks or called to account. In the case of Kuwait, the UN had simply issued a mandate to liberate the tiny state from illegal occupation; nothing further was contemplated. This enabled the Americans to break off military action once the bare terms of this mandate had been fulfilled, and to withdraw with as few losses as possible just when the toppling of Saddam was within reach.

It is an unavoidable fact of political life in the United States, and therefore also of international events, that an American president's first four-year term of office is dedicated to securing his re-election. At the time of the Gulf War, President Bush had not yet been re-elected to a second term. Bush had to assume that the pursuit of Saddam Hussein would be both lengthy and costly in terms of American blood. It was logical to anticipate that Bush would find himself forced to justify ever-increasing US casualty lists to the electors at home. Public campaigns to end the war would gain in strength as the casualty figures mounted, with the cry to 'bring our boys home' growing ever louder and more penetrating. The American public seemed both mesmerized and even traumatized by the experience of Vietnam. It looked as though the price of pushing on into Iraq to force Saddam from power would be the rejection of Bush by the US electorate. Bush had to fear the same situation which had faced his predecessors Johnson and Nixon, both of whom had been forced to endure a veritable storm of opposition in the face of lengthening casualty lists from Vietnam.

To avoid such unpopularity, Bush contented himself with leaving Saddam's dictatorship in place. Overthrowing the régime would have required a thrust through Iraq at least as far as Baghdad, undoubtedly in the face of very tough resistance and with commensurate losses. To secure Bush a further four years in the White House, it was thought appropriate to leave Saddam Hussein to continue his reign of terror. There was relief all round that significantly fewer casualties had been sustained than had been estimated, and feared, before the action began. The ironic thing was that Bush in any case failed to secure re-election, whereas on the other hand the total defeat and elimination of Saddam Hussein would probably have ensured him this.

A job left half-done – and for this, American transport aircraft alone had flown 482,000 people and 513,000 tons of freight across the Atlantic into the Gulf region – the equivalent of moving the entire populations of both Wolverhampton and Dundee, together with all their foodstuffs, motor vehicles and the contents of their homes, one-third of the way round the globe.

Declining to go any further than the simple UN mandate to liberate Kuwait was excused with the hollow explanation that one does not intervene in the internal affairs of other states – not even to put an end to Saddam's slaughter of the Kurds. With the same spurious reasoning about internal affairs one could have declined in the winter of 1944/45 to push into Germany itself, being content with driving out the *Wehrmacht* from the countries which it had occupied. Such excuses for neglecting to finish off Saddam Hussein convince no one. The plain truth is that a wider-reaching mandate was simply not wanted from the UN.

The Americans displayed no such inhibitions about intervening in the internal affairs of Grenada (1983) and Panama (1989), there being on those occasions no high price in blood likely to be exacted. It was clear that American interests were threatened in Panama, leading that same President Bush to order US troops into invasion for the high-sounding 'Operation Just Cause'.

On the other hand, the attempted genocide of Kurds, not threatening US interests, merited no such attention. It appears not to have been grasped, even after twenty centuries of the Christian era, that genocide is not an internal affair of any state, but rather something which is everyone's business. If ever there was a just cause during Bush's presidency, rescuing the Kurds was it. It had been Bush's own words *('We hope that the Iraqi people will rise to eject Saddam Hussein')* which had encouraged the Kurds to offer some resistance to the brutal Iraqi régime. Later, the Kurds were to feel that the West had let them down. This episode echoes Soviet conduct outside Warsaw in 1944, when the approaching Red Army used radio to call on the population of the Polish capital to rise against the German forces of occupation, only itself to remain stationary outside the city, watching while the Germans systematically destroyed all Polish resistance.

One thing has to be conceded about Washington's crass neglect: a number of Saddam Hussein's neighbours hoped, and are still hoping, for him to be toppled. Should Iraq be eliminated as a danger to peace, Iran and Syria are likely to compete for the leading role in the Near and Middle East. Such a development could become as dangerous to stability in the region as Saddam's naked aggression.

Such considerations will have played no little part in Western calculations at the time of the Gulf War. Both before and during the military action, Western spokesmen stressed repeatedly that there was neither desire to wage war on the Iraqi people nor any intention of stripping Iraq of territory. Doubtless these assurances concerning Iraq's territorial integrity were rooted in the recognition that any excessive weakening of the Iraqi state would allow too much freedom for the long-standing expansionist dreams of both Iran and Syria, thus only creating the potential for further conflicts.

In order to keep one's own losses to a minimum, it is essential first to conduct a preparatory air assault for as long as possible before going over to forward movement on the ground. Such partially 'hands off' warfare goes a little way along the road envisioned by those first theoreticians of strategic air war. It is a part confirmation of the concept, but at the same time misleading.

The most significant legacy of the Gulf War must be just those self-delusory dreams which have been wakened in Western minds by the apparently easy success of the 'smart weapons' which were directed accurately to their targets. These devices do not allow a true 'hands off' mode of warfare; this is not yet in sight. What is generally overlooked is the simple fact that, as also with every other type of arm, the seeds of an effective counter-weapon are intrinsic in the very nature of 'smart weapons'. Against the throwing or the stabbing device, defenders had the helmet, the armour, the shield; against machine guns, the trench; against bombs and shells the concrete bunker. Against computer-guided missiles there are electronic counter-measures. The task of jamming or breaking down the other fellow's guidance signals is a matter of routine for every electronics expert working in the defence field.

Despite the initial success of 'smart weapons', it remains a fact that while the Americans claimed eighty per cent accuracy of their Tomahawk cruise missiles in the Gulf, only fifty per cent of the Tomahawks launched reached their intended targets. In many cases, either the motor or the gyroscope failed; other Tomahawks were simply shot down in flight.

During the war, Saddam Hussein allowed the outside world a further glimpse of his true character and a vision of the sort of warfare which Western peoples can expect in conflicts with states led by less humane régimes. Among the nightmares threatened by such governments are terrorist actions within the countries of their opponents and the arrest of foreign nationals for detention at sites of military importance which could be targets for the enemy (the building of so-called 'human shields').

Saddam also tried to extend the war, or alternatively to break up the alliance formed against him, by firing SCUD rockets against Israel. Involving Israel was intended to secure the departure of Syria, Egypt and Saudi Arabia from the alliance. Had Saddam succeeded in provoking Israel into a military response, he might have been in a position to expand the conflict into an Islamic *Jihad*, or holy war. Saddam could be sure that Arab nations would never fight alongside Israel against an Islamic Arab 'brother'. When the SCUD attacks on Israel failed to achieve the intended effect (the Israelis fought off the rockets but launched no answering assaults),

Saddam tried another trick. He made a false announcement that American aircraft had attacked two holy Islamic shrines. This item of misinformation was likewise intended to secure the exit of Arab states from the anti-Iraq alliance, and if possible to persuade them to switch sides. Here, too, the attempt failed.

When driven from Kuwait, the Iraqis made reality of another nightmare with which they had threatened. They blew up and set fire to Kuwait's oilfields as they went. Even before the Allies had begun their military operations, Iraqi forces had prepared for this sabotage by mining many of the thousand or so oil wells in the occupied country. Even though defeated militarily, the Baghdad régime might by these means still have achieved one of its foreign policy objectives: eliminating Kuwait as a rival oil supplier, with consequent price rises. Any such aim will have been effectively frustrated by the subsequent oil export embargo imposed on Iraq.

Half of the world's oil reserves have already been consumed in the course of little more than a century of motorization. It is apparent that the remainder will be exhausted during the next few decades. Half of all remaining supplies are in the Middle East; once alternative fuels (such as hydrogen) are in general use, oil will cease to be a factor in world affairs and the industrial world will have no further need to kowtow to anyone in the region.

Basic questions remain: Why was the secretary-general of the United Nations not in Baghdad repeatedly during the Gulf crisis of 1990/91? Why was it left to American statesmen and diplomats to make all the efforts to resolve the matter before taking military action?

The world at the start of a new century

GORBACHEV'S LEGACY

A frequently heard complaint is that no attention was paid to Hitler's early announcement of his objectives. Hitler, it is pointed out with complete accuracy, had published his aims in the mid-1920s in the two volumes of his book *Mein Kampf* (My Struggle), yet none of his opponents had taken these seriously. Almost no one had taken the trouble even to read *Mein Kampf*.

These are perfectly understandable objections. Yet if they are to be regarded as justifiable criticism of the statesmen of those days, then the least that can be said is that the same deficiencies were detectable among the Western leaders of the 1980s *vis-à-vis* the policies and intentions of Mikhail Gorbachev. What Gorbachev was attempting had already been practised by Lenin as far back as 1921, and explained in unequivocal language in Kremlin publications. Few things are easier than for those interested to put themselves in the picture about all this. All major historical annals, as well as the collected or selected works of Lenin, which have been printed in enormous numbers out of all proportion to their importance, testify that what Gorbachev was attempting was nothing new.

The *perestroika* of the Gorbachev era, that dramatic series of turns-round in the Kremlin's foreign and domestic policies, was nothing more than a return to one of Lenin's tried and proven strategies – what the first Soviet dictator had himself described as *'howling with the wolves'*. Deliberately putting a temporary end to the original militant form of communism, Lenin brought about a revival of the Soviet economy by reintroducing a degree of market economy (the *New Economic Policy*). This provided a powerful springboard for the *New Socialist Offensive* which was to follow under Stalin in 1928. Gorbachev pursued the same scheme in introducing 'counter-revolutionary' measures with the object of strengthening communism. In doing so, he opened Pandora's box. It is certain that Gorbachev never expected his reforms to go so far. What he as a convinced communist wanted was clear enough; what he brought about was something quite different. The removal of communists from power was not part of his plan; Gorbachev simply wanted to succeed where his predecessors had failed. Lenin had been thwarted in his efforts to incite world revolution. Stalin had not managed to conquer the non-Soviet world by military force.

Gorbachev, however, succeeded in persuading the free West to disarm, creating the preconditions for possible later Russian annexations in Europe. Overrunning Europe may now no longer be part of Moscow's plans, but all the same, Gorbachev's legacy is not a safer, but a more dangerous world.

The world has been destabilized by Gorbachev through his putting an end to the generally feared 'balance of terror'. As long as there was an approximately equal balance of forces (and to deter aggression it is enough for there to *appear* to be a balance), it remained certain that the Soviets would risk no military adventures in Europe. By destroying this guarantee of European and world peace, Gorbachev turned both Europe and the world into an unstable powder keg. Paradoxically, there is such a thing as peace through confrontation. This is achieved, as experience shows, when only two comparably strong opponents face one another directly (i.e., NATO and the Warsaw Pact).

Wars break out far more easily through multiple confrontations. The non-existence of European alliances of unmistakably equal strength undoubtedly contributed to the outbreak of war in 1939, while on the other hand it was the very multiplicity of mutual pacts and treaties before 1914 which had then made a major conflict practically inevitable. Similar weaknesses were a factor during Napoleon's wars; the French emperor was a master at playing off the countries of Europe against one another. It is apparent that the equilibrium necessary to maintain peace cannot be a permanent state. Since international relationships are dynamic by nature, the situation is continually moving either towards or away from a state of equilibrium. As long as these movements take place within acceptable limits (like the variations of exchange rates between international currencies), peace can be maintained.

During the so-called 'Cold War', the general fear of war itself was so great that significantly greater displacements than usual were tolerated in the relationships between major states – this tolerance admittedly accompanied by much grinding of teeth, but with the disharmonies nonetheless accorded tacit acceptance. Among western peoples, at least, it was never possible for the customary cartoon-like hostile view of the other side, that image built on fear and exaggeration, to take firm root in the imagination. The public mind was dominated by fear not of conquest by the Soviets, but of nuclear war with the Soviets.

Direct confrontation and fear kept the peace for half a century. These stabilizing factors have now been removed. In the world as destabilized by Gorbachev, Third World (non-aligned) states can no longer be restrained by the great powers. Pre-Gorbachev, the USA and the Soviet Union had reason to fear that conflicts in the Third World could escalate into a world war. As a result, governments in Washington and Moscow took care to prevent their client states from going off the rails. For this purpose, it was sufficient for the great powers to use the weight of their military or economic power. The threat not to deliver any replacement supplies of arms or ammunition was one of the commonest means applied to dissuade a nation armed with US or Soviet equipment from indulging in military adventures which might have dragged in the great powers to face one another. These means of preserving peace are no longer available, thanks to the collapse of the Soviet power structure brought about unwittingly by Gorbachev. Without Moscow's restraining hand, several developing countries are threatening to run out of control. Before Gorbachev's upheavals, Moscow would for instance have had little difficulty in preventing Iraq from invading Kuwait. In stark contrast, the Kremlin's special envoy, Yevgeni Primakov, flew in vain to Baghdad in the autumn of 1990 with a demand for Iraqi troops to be withdrawn from Kuwait. As though Russia's gigantic military power had been rendered impotent at a stroke, Primakov had to return to Moscow to report abject failure – an outcome unthinkable in pre-Gorbachev days.

While weak and only moderately armed states are condemned by their lack of strength to annihilation whenever it shall please almighty powers to destroy them, major actors on the world stage tend to eliminate themselves in time through the ever-increasing cost of waging wars to maintain their position. The breakup of the Soviet Union must be unique in world history, since this is one collapse of a great empire which was brought about not by exhaustion in war but simply through the cost of an arms race in peacetime!

RUSSIA

The Soviet Union was probably the first state in world history to have armed itself to death rather than fighting itself into the grave. Moscow's empire was bankrupted by its excessive arms race expenditure. According to Gorbachev's own figures, the Kremlin devoted some twenty-five per cent of the Soviet Union's gross national product to military purposes.

While Soviet soldiers and weapons were being withdrawn from Eastern and Central Europe amid a mass of publicity, the Soviet Union under Gorbachev was building nine new attack submarines in a period of only eighteen months (between spring 1992 and autumn 1993). By comparison, it should be recalled that Germany started the Second World War with a total of only twenty-nine diesel-powered U-boats; Gorbachev's fleet numbered twelve times this number, many of them nuclear-powered. The submarine is now, of course, *the* carrier of today's strategic weapons. She can lie in wait anywhere in the world's seas and oceans, and her long-range rockets can be fired underwater to reach any point on earth.

The Soviet Union deployed a total of some 27,000 nuclear warheads. On the break-up of the monolithic state, these were distributed as follows: ca. 19,000 remained in Russia; Ukraine received ca. 4,000; Kazakhstan ca. 1,800; and Belarus ca. 1,250. A further thousand remained deployed at sea and elsewhere. The majority of warheads still extant in the Ukraine, Kazakhstan and Belarus are fitted to short-range missiles. In addition to her arsenal of action-ready weapons, Russia still possesses stocks of an estimated 1,500 tons of plutonium and enriched uranium.

In 1987, the Soviet Union possessed 1,418 intercontinental rockets; in 1996 Russia had 800. Of 360 Soviet submarines, Russia retains 183; of 274 large warships, only 152. A 165-strong fleet of strategic bombers has shrunk to one of eighty-six in Russian hands. Out of 53,300 tanks in the Soviet Army, Russia's rulers now have 16,800; instead of an army of five millions, only one million men.

These remain formidable forces. When Russia's representatives agreed in May 2000 to the UN proposal to scrap atomic arms, there was of course no mention of any timetable for implementation. Russian tactical nuclear weapons, stored at more then 200 different locations, can be delivered to their targets by artillery pieces or short-range rockets which are in the hands of more than 140 divisions as standard equipment. They can be carried in more than 3,000 aircraft and on almost all ships of the states of the former Soviet Union.

The world's largest assemblage of strategic and tactical nuclear weapons, warplanes and naval forces can be found at the Kola Peninsula on Russia's Arctic coast. Under Gorbachev, the most westerly of Russia's airfields for heavy bombers was built on the southern half of the peninsula, its three-miles-long main runway designed for take-off in attacks chiefly on Britain and the USA. Also under Gorbachev, a gigantic naval harbour with submarine base was built some 200 miles to the east of Murmansk, on Kola's northern coast. This is home to the world's largest submarine type, the Typhoon. Each of these 30,000-ton monsters is capable of launching twenty SS-N-20 nuclear rockets over a distance of 5,000 miles without herself sailing far out into the world's oceans.

Russia's armed forces were built up according to a principle of Lenin's: *'Quantity is quality in itself'*. During the Second World War, the Red Army always fought from a position of massive numerical superiority and was nonetheless obliged to suffer horrendous defeats. In Afghanistan, the Russians discovered that their massed motorized divisions could not be deployed effectively. As a result of these experiences, they have gone over to mixed formations, consisting of mechanized groups and smaller units transported by helicopter.

Gorbachev's reforms have unleashed unexpected difficulties founded in the lack of personnel quality. Even the reliability of the armed services as internal forces of order has been called into question. KGB and NVD troops (from the State Security Service and the Interior Ministry) are normally used to quell civil disturbances. Should there be simultaneous risings in several republics, these forces would be overstretched and would have to ask for assistance from the Army. The success of any such deployment would be jeopardized by the current catastrophic morale within the armed services, the situation being still further threatened by the effects of ethnic disturbances within Army units.

Though the Russian people still command enormous military power, they are starting the twenty-first century in a state of psychological depression, experiencing severe national distress at the loss of their gigantic empire. All the same, Russia still possesses three-quarters of the land area of the former Soviet Union, with a population of 150 millions. Some seventy per cent of the 290 million former Soviet citizens live in the three core republics of the new Community of Independent States: Russia, Belarus and the Ukraine. Outside Russia itself, some twenty-five million Russians live in newly independent peripheral states. Should these feel that they are becoming a repressed minority, they could supply a reason for nationalist Russian intervention. No one is likely to wish the Russians to have still more fighting on their territory. People and state both need as long a period as possible of economic and social stability. Meanwhile, officers who have been discharged as part of the run-down of Russian forces are being given occupational retraining at the expense of the British taxpayer.

THE STATES OF THE FORMER WARSAW PACT

An agreement of unusual interest was concluded in 1994 between the Ukraine and the United States, providing for payment of one million US dollars 'per head' against the dismantling of 1,800 of the nuclear warheads left on Ukrainian territory by Soviet forces. The Ukraine had inherited the world's third largest nuclear arsenal, after those of Russia herself and the United States.

Some 1,500 of the nuclear weapons deployed in the Ukraine had been programmed against targets in the USA. It was therefore no surprise that the Americans were prepared to pay a million dollars for every dismantled warhead. The 1.8 billion dollars accruing from this arrangement were intended to help resurrect the Ukrainian economy ruined by the communist régime, with the nuclear materials yielded from dismantling forwarded to the Americans for reprocessing.

The breakup of the Soviet Union and the dissolution of the Warsaw Pact has allowed long-suppressed tensions and animosities between the peoples of the former alliance to come to the to surface. Hungary for example is outraged at the treatment and status of Hungarian minorities in Slovakia and Romania. The twenty-five million or so Russians now living as minorities in the newly independent peripheral states of the former USSR also threaten potential problems: Kazakhstan's population is thirty-eight per cent Russian, Latvia's thirty-four per cent and Estonia's thirty per cent, while the Ukraine and Kirghizia each have twenty-two per cent Russians.

The actions of Russian forces against Chechnya are well enough known. Since the dissolution of the Soviet multi-state, Russian troops have also intervened in fighting between Armenia and Azerbaijan, as well as in Moldova, Georgia and Tadjikistan. To justify any similar actions in the peripheral states, it will probably be enough for Moscow to cite the need for shielding Russian minorities.

Several countries in eastern Europe have already expressed a wish to live under the protection of the West. As a result, the Western response to dissolution of the Warsaw Pact is unlikely to be the winding-up of NATO, but rather its further expansion. Military cooperation has already started.

Hungary has requested British help in building up her armed forces. British military experts who travelled to Hungary to assess the country's armed services and to begin a programme of improvements were astonished to have been initiated at once into all the secrets of the Budapest defence ministry.

Poland, Latvia and the Ukraine are also, like Hungary, anxious to acquire British military expertise. High-ranking officers of the Ukrainian army have already attended courses at British military institutions. Romania and Poland have been looking for the help of British experts in modernizing and strengthening their forces. Large-scale training programmes have been conducted by British soldiers in Poland, whose army is particularly keen to acquire British expertise in tank warfare.

On achieving their independence from Moscow, Latvia's leaders even asked the London government to appoint a British officer as overall commander-in-chief of Latvian forces. For diplomatic reasons, London suggested that the officer detailed should function nominally only as second-in-command. A Royal Artillery colonel was accordingly posted to Riga as deputy commander-in-chief of the 7,000 men of Latvia's army and her 16,500-strong militia.

Such developments are likely to worry Russia's nationalist and surviving communist circles. Demands have already been made for the Russian-Ukrainian border to be secured, and there is anxious talk that Poland's frontiers might be moved eastwards. The territories of the Warsaw Pact had of course served Russia as a *cordon sanitaire sovietique*.

NATO

NATO's reaction to the demise of the Warsaw Pact was to throw overboard its doctrine of 'flexible response', which had been valid since 1967, without adopting any new basic approach to its responsibilities. There has been considerable discussion about a range of possible troop dispositions, including:

multinational defence forces with the latest electronic early warning systems, deployed in Germany to guard the gateway to western Europe;

highly mobile, multinational 'rapid reaction forces', which in emergency could race to the assistance of forces on German soil;

highly mechanized troops in reserve, which could be drawn from further NATO countries in times of crisis. These would consist chiefly of reservists, being mobilized only once a crisis had arisen.

A study undertaken jointly by the National Security Council of the USA and the German Defence Ministry foresees the following three stages of future crises, without naming a potential enemy:

'persuasive measures', i.e., coordinated political and military steps: diplomatic pressure, mobilization and the despatch of ACE units (Allied Command Europe) into the crisis area;

in the event that 'persuasion' should fail, limited use of nuclear weapons with the object of deterring the other side from escalating the conflict;

should these measures also fail, total atomic war.

It remains unclear how far any limited use of nuclear weapons is supposed to extend. There is certain to be disagreement among NATO countries. Many European governments may well consider the use of a single nuclear weapon, for example against an enemy missile site in a thinly-populated area, to be sufficient to bring about a political settlement of any confrontation. The more realistic British and Americans, on the other hand – and perhaps even the

French – will certainly see no point in doing less than simultaneously destroying a number of targets critical to the enemy.

It is equally unclear what means might be thought effective in preventing the first use of nuclear weapons from escalating at once into full-scale atomic war.

No less mysterious are the nature and extent of the military measures expected to 'persuade' – or dissuade – a potential aggressor before the limited use of nuclear weapons is seen to be necessary. The plain, and generally unknown, fact is that of all NATO member countries only Britain and the USA are capable of despatching even a single complete division, ready to fight, anywhere outside their own borders.

No aggressor will be 'persuaded' by passive defence of one's own homeland, such as that for which most European forces – even the German *Bundeswehr* – are equipped and trained. This means that an early transition to the second stage use of nuclear weapons will be unavoidable. Without adequate forces available on the ground *before* a crisis erupts, the anticipated three stages can rapidly become telescoped into the single step directly into full-scale atomic war.

While the forces stationed in Europe by both NATO and the former Warsaw Pact have been run down, various possibilities have been considered for new NATO dispositions, among them:

> creation of forward operations bases in Germany for NATO aircraft, presently stationed outside Germany, armed with nuclear weapons;
> transfer of nuclear artillery shells to Germany in times of crisis;
> establishment of a rapid reaction force consisting of six divisions with a total of 100,000 men.

Of course, should nuclear weapons actually be scrapped, the western countries will be left with absolutely nothing with which to deter or 'persuade' any stronger power.

There appear to be no plans to tackle the permanent problem of non-standardization of weapons and equipment among the armed forces of NATO member countries. NATO has been in existence for more than fifty years, yet still not all warships in the alliance are able to refuel in all naval harbours; not all military aircraft can be serviced at all airfields.

It is scarcely necessary to remark that Warsaw Pact forces never had to struggle against stupidity and incompetence of this kind.

NATO must treat as its top-priority task the development and deployment of the much-discussed SDI shield (Strategic Defence Initiative), covering not just North America but Europe as well.

As is well enough known, the basis of the NATO Treaty is that each member state commits itself to regarding any attack on another member state as an attack upon itself. This means that if any single NATO member becomes the victim of an assault, all the other member states are obliged to join in war against the aggressor.

Poland, Hungary and the Czech Republic have already been accepted into NATO, while a number of other former Warsaw Pact members have likewise expressed their interest in joining: Estonia, Latvia, Lithuania, Slovakia, Romania, Bulgaria, Macedonia, Albania and Slovenia. NATO has made an offer to Russia of military cooperation, but Moscow has declined, preferring instead to cultivate closer direct links with individual NATO countries.

It is above all the smaller peripheral states, such as Latvia, who are hoping for effective protection for their newly won independence through membership in NATO. They have not been backward in drawing attention to official Russian pronouncements making them fear re-annexation.

As time goes by, such an eventuality may appear to become less likely. All the same, a re-awakening of imperialistic Russian nationalism cannot be ruled out for ever. Should Latvia, for example, indeed be annexed by Russia, the consequence of NATO membership of the tiny Baltic state would be that all NATO countries would be drawn automatically into war with Russia.

The newly created democracy in Russia and in the states of eastern Europe is by no means firmly established. The upheavals of 1989 made Europe and the world order less stable.

Before accepting new members, it is essential for the peoples of NATO countries to ask themselves seriously:

first, whether they are prepared to go to war – if necessary to fight a nuclear war – to defend the independence of one of these eastern European states;

second, whether they understand that any attempt from western Europe to liberate one of Russia's small neighbouring countries from occupation by Russian forces would be filled with enormous military difficulties and would probably cost more lives than the entire population of the country concerned;

third, whether the Kremlin would not be likely to regard any acceptance into NATO of one of these peripheral states as a direct challenge, whether such a step is not likely to lead to tensions between Russia and the West, and whether it would not be better to strive for closer and deeper relations with Russia, rather than undertaking any possibly provocative steps which could lead to a return to the 'Cold War'.

It is necessary only to recall the Franco-British guarantee to Poland in 1939, which proved not only militarily unenforceable but appeared to act on Hitler as a direct challenge, provoking rather than deterring him.

Ignoring any such sensible reflections, President Clinton took it on himself – as though NATO were a matter for the United States alone – to make a personal proclamation of 1999 as the year for accepting new NATO member states. Washington circles confirmed this choice of year, without naming any more militarily sound reason than that 1999 would see the fiftieth anniversary of the alliance's foundation!

This is the sort of monstrous simple-mindedness with which decisions are made potentially determining life and death for countless millions. As long as there remains no requirement that a candidate for the highest political office demonstrate either wisdom or insight, we all remain likely to 'slip into war' once again.

EUROPE

Over the weekend of October 13/14, 1990, the European Union announced in Venice that it wished to investigate the possibility of running its own defence policy. This would mean that the EU would one day maintain its own armed forces with a central command structure. The proposal was discussed further at EU 'summit' meetings in Portugal in June 2000.

It will not work.

Both the EU and the European Parliament have spent the years of their existence so far demonstrating their total incapacity for solving problems which compared with those life-and-death matters implicit in foreign policy and defence are relatively unimportant.

Europe is vulnerable to threat from outside because, among other things, it is much more dependent on overseas trade than its competitors. The USA is the world's greatest economic power, yet foreign commerce accounts for only some five per cent of her total trade. Even Japan, with her position as the leading supplier of manufactured goods, depends on overseas business for only ten per cent of her economy. Britain, on the other hand, relies on foreign trade for twenty per cent of her turnover; in Germany's case, the proportion is no less than one quarter. The member states of the European Union by themselves import one fifth of all the world's agricultural produce. At least the necessity of defending ocean routes ought to penetrate European heads and lead to recognition of the necessity of adopting some kind of joint strategic defence concept. Yet for any such collective scheme to be created, certain European peoples would first have radically to alter their attitudes towards their neighbours. Piously expressed intentions will achieve nothing on their own.

The 'constitution' of the European Union, the Treaty of Rome, forbids the union to concern itself with military matters. This is certain to be changed, though some countries – such as Denmark, which has always contributed only the bare minimum to NATO activities – would prefer to leave things as they are. Greece, too, is unlikely to show much enthusiasm, while neutral Ireland always wants to plough a lone furrow. The entry of the Irish Republic to the EU was arranged only by granting special conditions to the Dublin government. Whenever defence matters are touched on at the EU, Ireland's representatives make an ostentatious exit from the chamber. From the beginning, Dublin governments have always rejected either membership in NATO or making any contribution to collective defence of Europe.

Peoples who are unable to conquer their own old prejudices – and there are many such in western Europe alone – are totally unsuitable as partners in any military alliance. The conduct over the years of the representatives and governments of Britain's European 'partners' leaves not the slightest room for doubt that they are congenitally incapable of considering anyone's interests other than their own. It is impossible to imagine these self-centred peoples making the resources available to create the common strategic missile defences which are the absolute minimum of what is essential.

The EU Council of Ministers has been charged with drawing up a list of those foreign policy and military problems thought appropriate for the EU to tackle. After the Venice meeting, the first steps were taken towards formulating a joint foreign policy – from which military action, when necessary, must spring. Just as the Europeans were preparing for this significant step, they flopped. When forces were sought for the liberation of Kuwait, most European states could be persuaded to provide only financial and non-military assistance (medical facilities, transport and the like).

In their reluctance to participate, the prosperous Europeans were put to shame by Afghanistan and even by the small African state of Senegal, both of these poor countries contributing fighting men. Pakistan and Bangladesh each also sent troops, but that much-trumpeted child of European integration, the joint Franco-German brigade, was not despatched to the Gulf. Too many European governments and peoples made it abundantly apparent that they were more than ready to stand by and watch the aggression of a ruthless dictatorship without themselves lifting a finger to help the victims. To tie one's own hands in treaties with any such nations is tantamount to national suicide. Perhaps fearful of terrorist retaliation by Iraq, Belgium refused to supply Britain with small arms ammunition for her troops in the Gulf. French forces despatched to Saudi Arabia took up positions well away from their British and American allies, demonstrating an ostentatious independence of joint Allied command. How are such people, some of whom have evidently forgotten what it is like to be occupied themselves by an invader, supposed to make a common European defence policy work?

To close observers of Europe, none of the above could come as a surprise. A 'World Values Survey' conducted during the 1980s identified fundamental differences between Britain and her Continental 'partners'. Whereas in the UK and the USA there was overwhelming affirmation that individual freedoms were valued more highly than any notion of personal 'equality', a clear majority of Germans, Italians and Spanish left no doubt that feeling themselves to be 'equal' to others was most important to them, with freedom for the individual insignificant in their scale of values.

No state or society can prove sustainable unless its laws and the conduct of its affairs are structured around a single aggregation of values. Adherence to varying dietary customs dictated by religious beliefs do not undermine a society, but ingrained differences in appreciation of which values are to be defended by waging war are certainly capable of destroying it. The fashionable concept of 'multicultural' societies is doomed to be short-lived. Any such notions will collapse as soon as lethal threats to society become apparent from outside.

There is now talk of establishing a 60,000-strong European 'rapid reaction' force, despite the fact that the only reaction natural to most in the European Union is to duck (they are, admittedly, very rapid at that). Her European 'partners', with their record of rolling over onto their backs to please whichever dictator holds sway at the moment, would never join Britain in united opposition to a determined assault. Rather than link her fortunes to peoples who appear to think that whoever shouts loudest must be right, and that personal survival is the highest goal in life, Britain would do infinitely better were she to rejoin her former American colonies. As the latest addition to the United States, Britain would enjoy a freedom increasingly denied her by the intolerant dictatorships of Strasbourg and Brussels. The British would find that they have inexpressibly more in common with their new transatlantic fellow-citizens than with their nearer neighbours. This course is not necessarily advocated; the possibility is mentioned to emphasize the warning against British submergence in a European straitjacket state.

As a *raison d'être* for the establishment of a European Community, the wish to abolish warfare from European life was thoroughly understandable and justifiable. The founders of the movement towards European integration acted perfectly reasonably in their reaction of horror after the experiences of the devastating wars of the first part of the twentieth century. They took the view that commonality of essential economic interests would prevent the outbreak of rivalries and envy. The thinking was right, and for centuries had been more than overdue in Europe.

Even so, these good intentions had already been realized *de facto* even as their *de jure* framework was being formulated. Fifty years on, this framework must be considered long obsolete. The fact is that the peoples of Europe had by 1945 already recognized war as self-mutilation, and needed no politicians to tell them so or to found any artificial institutions. Since then, the familiarity between peoples engendered by regular international travel has served only to reinforce this state of affairs. At least among West Europeans, the thought of going to war against one another ever again has meanwhile become as unthinkable, even as laughable, as war between Scots and English.

To live in peace alongside one another, to mix with a minimum of hindrance and restriction, to be good neighbours – this is what the peoples of Europe want. The nations of this continent, the wellspring of all human progress, want to live together in harmony, and they will live together in harmony. They will manage to tolerate one another, and despite all their contrasting values and characteristics they will no longer fly at each other's throats. This is all a state which has been attained spontaneously, without the interference of any politician. On the other hand, any attempt to force through political integration can set back this felicitous development. Compulsory union can revive ancient resentments between peoples who at present live as good neighbours *alongside* one another, but do not necessarily wish to live *with* one another in the same house. We have seen how Croatians, Bosnians and other nationalities are prepared to be killed rather than live together in the same state with Serbs. Czechs and Slovaks, who were not asked in 1919 whether they wished to be flung together into the same pot, have seized the first opportunity to break apart into their own individual republics. This ought to tell the Euro-enthusiasts something. Unmistakably the trend is towards national independence, to self-government within a people's own borders. The day of the supranational state is over.

The eagerness with which independence has been grasped by so many peoples constitutes an unequivocal warning: that a European Union forced into being as a unified state could tend to encourage fighting, rather than prevent it. The feeling of belonging to *one* particular people and to no other lies deep within the human psyche. Britain's Foreign Secretary Robin Cook was forced to acknowledge this out of his experiences with the dismantled Yugoslavia. *'Ethnic hatred runs deep, and we have been unable to eradicate it'*, he admitted on BBC Radio 4 in February 2000.

Disregarding the depth and intensity of such feelings has probably been the cause of more foreign policy 'own goals' than any other kind of miscalculation. For the European Union to repeat this error would provide merely another illustration of man's general incapacity to learn. Once they have set an idea into their heads, of course, politicians are well known for becoming blind to any kind of evidence contradicting it. But for this widespread antignosis, war would scarcely exist as a topic, and books such as this would never need to be written.

It ought to be a matter of course for every human automatically to structure his or her life so that as few areas of friction as possible can arise. Yet experience shows not only that too few people even bother to take this trouble, but that far too many actually enjoy conflict with their fellows. There are even some for whom confrontation becomes a full-time way of life. Probably everyone knows a person who is downright quarrelsome within the family or at his or her place of work, the one person without whose presence everyone else would manage along happily without any trouble.

Most people will have learned through hard experience that the only way to live with such a person is to give him or her right from the beginning no excuse to disturb other people's harmony. Such a type will in any case grumble when there is absolutely no reason to do so. Certain people are permanently looking for reasons to complain, and, of course, they can always find something. To play into the hands of such a person by supplying reasons for dissatisfaction is, put mildly, foolish. Statesmen should at least make the effort to manage both their internal societies and their international relations so as to eliminate as far as possible causes for dissatisfaction and friction. To programme the well-springs of trouble into state constitutions, as by forcing disparate peoples together into one unified state, must be regarded as nothing less than proof of total political incompetence – and dangerous incompetence, at that.

Implementing such far-reaching constitutional changes as union with another state can make sense only when these changes are supported by a convincing majority of the peoples concerned. It is of course best of all when the initiative for such a union originates in actual demands by the public.

The statesmen of the European Union call themselves democrats. They all claim that power resides in the people. If this is truly the case, then any initiatives towards European integration would have to follow popular demand. Just such demands are precisely what are missing in Europe; one wonders whether the statesmen ever even talk to the man in the street. The distinguishing feature of too many nominally democratic governments, with the honourable exception of the Swiss, is their persistent and arrogant refusal to implement the clearly expressed majority will of the people on numerous basic issues.

Any measure undertaken by government will be supported in the long run only when it enjoys the more or less tacit consent of the public. It is only thanks to implicit recognition of its justice and necessity that any law is supported, tolerated and – largely – obeyed by the broad mass of the people. Only a state constituted in conformity with the wishes and values of its citizens can survive. All laws and alterations to its constitution must stem from the will of the people; any measures forced on a people without this consent contains the seeds of society's destruction. Not to ask the people what they want, and to fling them together into a single state with others, according to one's own ideas, not theirs, is to repeat the errors of 1919, even though the consequences may not be as grave as they were in that particular case. Any such high-handed action has absolutely nothing to do with democracy and is no more than sheer dictatorship of the very kind which these so-called 'democrats' are so quick to condemn in others.

There can be scarcely a Euro-enthusiast who knows anything of the curious wartime provenance of the EU. The plan for a common market evolving via a single currency into a political entity was a child of Hitler's wartime planners. It provides an interesting example of efforts to comply with Clausewitz's exhortation not to lose sight of the political aims of a war *('The political aim is the end, war is the means, and the means should never be considered without the end')*.

A Nazi plan for a European Union under German domination was ready even before France had fallen in 1940. It was bequeathed to Hitler's successors in 1945, to be implemented despite Germany's defeat. The final step, the introduction of a common currency, is intended to lock everyone into the New Order in Europe without possibility of escape. *'In the year 2000, Europe will be a united continent'*, wrote Hitler's propaganda minister, Dr. Josef Goebbels, while he waited for Germany's final defeat. These were the opening words of his newspaper article published on January 30, 1945, under the heading *'If Germany should lose the war'*. Already there was no longer any *'if'*. Goebbels knew perfectly well that Germany was about to be defeated. With Germany's resources dwindling rapidly while she endured the sustained onslaught of millions of men and hundreds of thousands of heavy guns from both East and West, how could Goebbels know that Europe would become united despite the life being crushed out of the *Reich*? Had plans been laid, preparations met?

After Germany's unconditional surrender, her conquerors looked for 'werewolves', those expected Nazi fanatics who were supposed to fight on despite official capitulation. They found none. It was a sensational story at the time, and very widely believed. Not a newspaper in 1945 failed to report that fanatical Nazi troops were organized in so-called werewolf units which were going to carry on fighting even after Germany's unconditional surrender. The Third Reich might have been down, but it was not yet finally out. So, at least, very many people feared. As is well enough known, the threat proved to be imaginary. There was no protracted guerrilla warfare carried out from Alpine fortresses, no organized resistance to the occupying powers from among the defeated population. Germans, high and low, proved to be reassuringly docile and compliant. Obeying all orders of the Allied military governments, they seemed intent only on earnest rebuilding of their shattered homeland.

Were they perhaps *too* tractable? Were the werewolves perhaps not young men with rifles, submachine guns and hand grenades, after all, but simply sober, educated gentlemen wearing business suits with collars and ties? It was odd, really, that there should have been no armed resistance during the occupation. The Allies expected it. Many Germans certainly expected it. After all, the idea of triumphing despite defeat was central to Nazi thinking.

During Hitler's abortive Munich *Putsch* of 1923, seventeen Nazis were killed by police gunfire. A memorial erected to these 'martyrs' at the spot bore the inscription 'And you were nonetheless victorious' *(Und Ihr habt doch gesiegt)*. This phrase was known to every German. During the Third Reich, a permanent guard of honour was mounted at the memorial tablet, with every passer-by required to raise his right arm in the Nazi salute. This notion of an individual's dying in the assurance that his aims would be achieved despite personal destruction was a concept fundamental to the Nazi mentality. It was drummed into the heads of all members of the Hitler Youth – whose ranks included that arch-promoter of European unification, the recent German Chancellor Helmut Kohl. The boys' marching song, struck up on every possible occasion, promised: *'Germany will stand there radiant, even if we go under'*. With its final words, *'Yes, the flag is more than death'*, this anthem hammered into young German minds – Kohl's among them – the conviction that a political objective can outlive the individual.

Those who learned these words as youngsters cannot ever forget them. It has been the business of many of them since 1945 to see that Germany's ambition to dominate all of Europe is fulfilled despite that catastrophic defeat, that Germany should become 'nevertheless victorious', that Hitler's idea should prove 'more than death'. If his ambitions could not be implemented by force of arms, then by some other means.

There was much ironic joking then, and there has been plenty more since, about the 'thousand-year Reich' which managed to last for only twelve years. Perhaps, though, it is the Nazis who will after all have the last laugh – if the other peoples of Europe let them. It could have occurred to few people at the time that perhaps one or two clever Germans had thought out a surer way of realizing Nazi ambitions than through a continuation of the armed force which had already failed. Fully fifty years after Germany's defeat, we are confronted with a European Union developed according to the exact pattern drawn up by Nazi thinkers during the war. Coincidence or conspiracy? A study of Germany's wartime plans suggests that German longsightedness might have been under-estimated.

Over-confident to the point of self-delusion, Nazi planners had begun even before the conquest of France to map out Germany's route to domination of the continent. Europe was to be united to serve German interests; the method was to be stage-by-stage 'harmonization' of trade, taxation and currency, leading inevitably to final integration into a single state. The BEF was still defending its positions near the Channel coast when Werner Daitz, Director of

European Economic Planning in Berlin, completed his outline for a Common Market and European Union. His step-by-step design for the post-war world was dated May 31, 1940. Daitz warned that while the Germans were taking over the reins of other countries they must *'on principle speak only of Europe'*. He recognized that the best way to unite Europe under German rule was first to achieve regulation of the continent's trade, and then to create a common currency. This, via the Reichsbank, would effectively lock all countries into one single state run from Berlin.

Hitler's Finance Minister, Walther Funk, developed these ideas. By July 22, 1940, Funk was ready to tell his fellow-ministers that after the war Germany would organize a free exchange of goods between nations – preferably including Britain, but if necessary without. Alongside a customs union, said Funk, there would be a rational division of labour and an integrated structure for credit and balance of payments. Taxes, wages and prices would be coordinated and so would agriculture throughout Europe. Funk set up a working group which completed comprehensive plans for a European Economic Union. This same pattern of progressive integration devised by Funk's group has been implemented since the war, phase by phase:

> Southern Holland, Belgium, the Ruhr area, Luxembourg, Lorraine and Northern France were to be treated as one economic unit (the post-war 'European Coal and Steel Community');
>
> as a first step to European union, customs duties were to be abolished, then common tariffs imposed on goods imported into Europe from outside;
>
> stock market dealings would be regulated, restrictions on the circulation of capital lifted and vital economic information pooled;
>
> industry, trade and transport were to be rationalized (along the lines of the directives now issued by Brussels).

As prospects of German victory diminished, one might have expected Berlin's ambitions for unifying Europe to have been abandoned. Not a bit of it. Efforts to finalize plans were on the contrary intensified.

The over-confidence of the first years of war might have evaporated, but it was to be replaced by pragmatism. After the tide had turned unmistakably in 1943, Nazi Eurocrats worked harder than ever to refine a blueprint for post-war Europe which they could at least leave to their successors. It was as though a conscious decision had been made to abandon rape in favour of seduction, as promising a greater chance of lasting gratification.

By September 1943, the concrete framework for a 'European Union of States' had been drawn up in Ribbentrop's Foreign Office, whose official declaration of principles announced that *'Germany's war against Britain is the war of European unification'*.

This phrase will strike a chord with many in Britain, to whom the protagonists of European integration, our alleged 'partners', indeed seem, in every question from fishing quotas to subsidies for industry, to be waging war against Britain.

Examination of the way in which the European Union has evolved confirms that, ever since its inception, the European movement has followed slavishly at every stage the pattern of development laid down for it by its originators. Some will see it as a coincidence, but the fact is that the European movement has been and is being evolved along the precise lines envisaged by Nazi planners who outlined every stage of a post-war plan to unify Europe.

The abolition of customs duties, guaranteed prices for farmers, fishing regulated by quotas, common tariffs for imports from outside the union, one system of taxation common to every country, a passport headed 'European Community', a 'social chapter', a common currency – the recital sounds like a potted history of the EEC, the EC and the EU. Yet not one of these steps – not even the expression 'Common Market' or 'European Union' – is an idea which originated in Brussels or Strasbourg. Each was a part of the Clausewitzian 'political aim' with war as the means, every one devised in German ministries and think tanks during the war. In the event of a German victory, these plans would have been implemented at once; as things turned out, they were bequeathed to the Nazis' successors. Those who always suspected the European Union of being a sinister bureaucratic dictatorship will not be surprised to find that much of this step-by-step plan originated at SS Headquarters. It was in the SS's European Planning Office that designs were laid for measures which would survive a German defeat: for example, the plum-coloured European passport which has replaced our British one was dreamed up there in 1944.

During the war, the collaborationist leader of Vichy France, Pierre Laval, had said to Hitler: *'You want to win the war in order to unite Europe. Would it not be better to unite Europe in order to win the war?'* For those in the know, the feeling is inescapable that perhaps this is just what Hitler has succeeded in doing. Posthumously, for a posthumous Nazi victory. Instead of the Reichsbank in Berlin, it is the Central Bank in Frankfurt which is running EU economies. The name has changed, but the system and the aims are ones devised in 1940. Control people's money, and you control every aspect of their lives. Throughout history, empires which have subjugated others have imposed their own currency and taxation system on subject peoples. Unification of currency and taxation completes the military conquest. It will be remembered that monetary unity allowed Britain's American colonists no freedom of action, and that to break free from this financial and fiscal stranglehold they were compelled to fight a war for complete political independence.

The four powers ruling Germany after 1945 made the political division between East and West a reality by the simple device of creating separate German currencies, the eastern and western marks. By applying Daitz's scheme in reverse, to achieve the opposite effect, the Allies proved the efficacy of his thinking. So long as there were two distinct currencies, the two German states would remain independent of one another; a united currency, on the other hand, must lock people together. The first step necessary for the two German states to re-unite in 1991 was of course to re-establish a single currency.

Artur Axmann, Youth Leader of the German Reich, recorded a curious and perhaps significant remark made to him by Hitler in the Chancellery bunker when the German dictator said farewell before committing suicide. Asked by Axmann what was likely to be the future, after Germany's total military defeat, Hitler responded: *'Ideas live on according to laws of their own. I believe that something quite new will come'*. He did not elaborate.

Perhaps – but of course we can never know this – Hitler had in mind the European Union as the 'something quite new' which would arise in accordance with the laws allowing ideas to live on.

It is difficult to ignore the conviction that when the European Union becomes a political entity, this will be the birth of the Fourth Reich.

Britain's membership represents perverse rejection of an old saying. We could beat 'em, and still we joined 'em.

If the exact step-by-step implementation of the Nazi blueprint is mere chance, then this must be the greatest series of coincidences in history.

Political objectives have been achieved despite military defeat before this, principally through marriage between royal houses. Fulfilment of the defeated belligerent's plan through the voluntary actions of his former enemies must be unique, and could not have been foreseen even by Clausewitz's imaginative thinking.

THE UNITED KINGDOM

Because it has happened within living memory, Britain provides what for us is probably the clearest example of a state crippled by the cost and effort of fulfilling the world policing duties which it had taken upon itself.

As early as the mid-nineteenth century, when Britain was at the very height of her power, William Gladstone recognized the self-destructive senselessness of trying to leap in every time, everywhere, in an attempt to maintain world order. In a memorandum which he drew up for Queen Victoria when he first became Prime Minister in 1869, Gladstone asked:

> *'Is England so uplifted in strength above every other nation that she can with prudence advertise herself as ready to undertake the general redress of wrongs? Would not the consequences of such professions and promises be either the premature exhaustion of her means, or a collapse in the day of performance?'*

To avoid such disaster, Gladstone formulated the following golden rules for a realistic foreign policy:

> *'that England should keep entire in her own hands the means of estimating her own obligations;*
>
> *that she should not narrow her own liberty of choice by declarations made to other powers... of which they would claim to be at least joint interpreters;*
>
> *that, come what may, it is better for her to promise too little than too much;*
>
> *that she should not encourage the weak by giving expectations of aid to resist the strong, but should rather seek to deter the strong, by firm but moderate language, from aggressions on the weak'.*

Not only has every one of these principles been broken by Gladstone's successors; the realization of his fears is plain for all to see. Through her permanent duty as the world's policeman, Britain has done her best to finish herself off. This is something which all the great powers of the past have managed to do, the 'police actions' necessary to protect their possessions and interests finally ruining them economically. The same experience is likely to be made in time by the United States.

Despite this tendency, the invention of nuclear weapons has made it possible even for medium powers to deter or to fight off aggression without necessarily possessing either great wealth or massive human reserves. Any increase in the potency of arms raises the potential strength of the little fellow; it also tends to lengthen the distance from which he can strike at his enemy.

When battles were fought with man-to-man physical contact, a warrior could normally deal with only one opponent at a time – a fact of life conferring an automatic advantage on the side able to put more men into the field. A man with a revolver, on the other hand, is able to stand back a short way and take on six opponents. One with a machine gun can tackle a hundred over quite a distance. Strategic bombing, deploying modest numbers of aircrew, can decimate distant peoples. An ability to direct atomic weapons accurately to their targets raises the small nation's destructive potential out of all proportion to its physical mass or its resources.

At the beginning of the twentieth century, the British Empire encompassed one quarter of the earth's surface, namely 120 million square miles, with a total population approaching 400 millions. At the conclusion of the First World War, the Empire population had risen to 500 millions. A mere 5,000 British administrators managed to run India with her 290 millions, but the cost of military engagement on the sub-continent was to prove fatally weakening.

At the outbreak of the Second World War, Britain possessed more than forty-two per cent of the world's total merchant shipping tonnage. She was able to absorb horrendous losses to her merchant fleet without being knocked out of the fight, though the situation at sea did become what the Duke of Wellington would have called 'a damned close-run thing'. In crass contradistinction to this earlier life-preserving strength, Britain in 1990 was compelled to charter ships from other countries, in order to transport her forces to Saudi Arabia for the liberation of Kuwait.

In July 1996, Britain created a rapid reaction force with a core of 5,000 paratroopers and Royal Marines. Simultaneously, cuts in the defence budget brought down Army strength to its lowest level since the battle of Waterloo. In 1997 it fell below 100,000 for the first time in the post-Napoleonic period. Nonetheless, Britain's professional servicemen had earned themselves such a good reputation that, along with other countries, even France asked for the assistance of British officers in modernizing her own forces. After decades of military estrangement between the two peoples, renewed Franco-British comradeship had blossomed during their forces' joint actions in Bosnia. The British operating there had apparently impressed their cross-Channel neighbours with the quality of their officers, men, equipment and high level of training – to such an extent that in 1996 President Chirac made a public announcement of his government's intention of restructuring the French Army along the lines of the British.

As one century merges into another, British officers and expert personnel are helping to modernize the armed forces not only of France, but also of Poland, the Ukraine, Hungary and Romania. In addition, Latvia, Brunei, Oman and other small states have British officers 'on loan' in higher command positions.

For that six per cent of their gross national product which the British spend on defence (still only a sixth as much as their total bill for social security and health care), they enjoy the security ensured by versatile professional forces and a nuclear deterrent on a significant scale. Each of the sixty-four Trident II missiles carried on Britain's four nuclear-powered submarines has eight atomic warheads which can hit targets nearly 7,000 miles away with an accuracy of around one hundred yards. These weapons alone are capable of a nuclear assault on no fewer than 512 different targets.

A deterrent capable of making anyone stop and think! Yet the entire Trident system costs only as much as would two new armoured divisions – an increase in strength unlikely to deter any potential aggressor. Certainly, two armoured divisions can wreak a lot of havoc, but the sort of people likely to pose a serious threat to European powers will themselves be strong enough to be able to ignore such an additional factor with a superior smile. They will be able to allow that smile to develop into a full-blooded hearty laugh, should a British government really lose contact with reality to the extent of abandoning the UK's atomic arsenal. Such a step can be an option for a small country such as Britain only if her people are prepared without reservation one day to accept national and personal extinction.

Should they, on the other hand, wish to fight off any such threat, then the first thing that they will have to do if they abandon their nuclear weapons is to say farewell at the same time to most of the advantages of the modern welfare state. It has been possible to maintain the state-funded National Health Service, pensions, family allowances and all such benefits at the present levels thanks only to the savings in defence budget costs achieved through the bargain price of nuclear deterrence. There is scarcely anyone who would care to renounce the advantages of the welfare state – certainly not those very people who campaign most loudly against nuclear weapons. If we are to abandon these arms, non-nuclear forces will have to be built up to a factor of many times their present strength.

This would mean relinquishing many social benefits which we have hitherto enjoyed as of right. No democratic government, compelled to woo an electorate, is likely to undertake such a step. Yet we cannot have both: a high level of social benefits *and* adequate non-nuclear defence. There can be little doubt about the answer, were the public to be asked to choose between continuing to live under the nuclear umbrella with our present degree of social security and health care, or accepting the curtailment of these services in order to finance hugely increased non-nuclear forces – with, of course, compulsory military service something along the Swiss lines. Naturally, the question will never be put in that form. The illusion will be maintained that we can abandon our nuclear shield without bothering to increase our forces.

Let us attempt to determine what is required for national survivability.

The human body can sustain a considerable level of damage – lacerations, fractures, blood loss, amputations, disablements of one sort or another (such as the loss of an eye) – and will remain capable of life until vital organs such as heart, lungs or liver are put out of action. A nation, like the individual, is similarly dependent on a vital core of functions and strength which will keep it going despite severe losses. Part of this vital core is its physical ability to keep fighting, the remainder its moral determination to do so. It is this core which has to be the objective of all military undertakings. Destroy either the enemy's capacity to fight or his will to do so, and the war is over. It is not necessary to destroy both, but it certainly follows that one's military potency must be on a scale sufficient to inflict mortal damage on the enemy's moral and physical core. Our primary concern, if we wish to survive as a nation, has to be the question how we can inflict on an opponent that magnitude of destruction which will make him abandon the struggle – preferably before he begins it.

Thus far the situation is, one hopes, self-evident and capable of understanding even by an infant just entering school. Yet, horrifyingly, the plain fact is that almost everyone simply takes our armed forces for granted, never giving any conscious thought to the need for these to be given destructive power sufficient actually to knock out the other fellow. Most people merely assume in a vague sort of way that their country's forces will be able to deal with any eventuality, that they will fight off any assault and somehow be able to persuade the other fellow in the long run to lay down his arms. Cuts in armed forces strengths and in defence budgets are registered without reaction as just another news item – while expenditure to maintain an adequate level of arms brings in no votes to a government concerned above all other matters to be re-elected.

Human nature being as torpid as it is, narrow squeaks of the kind which Britain has survived in the past have not heightened our awareness of possible dangers, but have served only to induce in our good-natured people a comfortable, naïve assumption that we can always afford to let things slide and get away with it.

Recognition of the elementary is merely our starting point. We must attempt to see how in practice we can ensure that Britain's destructive power is adequate to shatter the other fellow's core.

Let us imagine a non-nuclear world in which Britain is opposed to a nation, say, four times larger than ourselves in land area, population, industrial production, raw material resources and so on. This imaginary land is home to people of strong moral fibre no less determined to defend their country than we ourselves. Moral factors equal, let us assume; physical considerations to the advantage of our opponent by a matter of four to one.

We may suppose from this that the enemy will have four times the physical resistance to our onslaughts that we have to his – remembering that total destruction of his vital core is not essential, the purpose in war being only to persuade the other side to ask for a cease-fire.

Other determinants being equal (such as the degree of resolution and skill with which both sides fight), we must assume that we should require four times our opponent's military strength in order to inflict on him the same level of damage which he can wreak on us. We are like a boxer facing four men in the ring, all punching him simultaneously. To cope, we are compelled to multiply both the numerical strength and the firepower of our armed forces.

Yet however much we increase our own military potency, the enemy will be able to do the same. He will always maintain, and can even extend, his quantitative ascendancy. Whatever we do, the nation significantly stronger in size and resources is always likelier to prevail. All exertion benefits the larger power, his greater mass generating an ever-widening linear superiority in his favour. As the process continues, so will the larger nation's margin of superiority rise. A calculating aggressor will in any case have increased his advantage from the start, by prior planning and effort.

All of this presupposes that the quality of the opposing armed forces is roughly equal, and that neither side suffers from any decisive shortage of fundamental materials such as nitrates for explosives, oil, steel, nickel, copper and so on. In this respect, Britain is not well blessed.

Let us now assume that at this point both sides acquire nuclear weapons, and, purely for the purposes of illustration, that these increase each nation's power of destruction by a factor of one hundred. This brings Carnoustie home to our opponent with a wallop.

Where he had been secure in an unmatchable superiority, suddenly we can warn him off with massive destructive potential. He might very well be in a position to reply with four times greater destruction, but so long as he is convinced that our strength is sufficient to overcome his vital core, he will not start anything.

Naturally, we cannot really quantify the toughness of the other fellow's core in order to fit it into a neat equation, but we can assess accurately enough the amount of damage which will render him incapable of waging war. It is apparent that a nuclear arsenal capable of inflicting this fatal destruction can abolish at a stroke the old advantages and disadvantages of size. A United Kingdom government which failed to maintain the available *ultima ratio* at a level of destructive potential capable of deterring the strongest power on earth would display hideous depths of criminal irresponsibility.

Of course, our own offensive capability is only half of the story. For a compact country like Britain, adequate ABM (anti-ballistic missile) defence is a *sine qua non*. So too is personnel quality.

Would-be recruits to the UK's armed forces now need to be put through six weeks of intensive physical fitness training before a selection can be made of those likely meet the minimum requirements attained with ease by earlier generations. This is all a result of sloppy upbringing, years wasted at schools where the authorities are afraid to make demands on the youngsters, an encouragement of obsession with self and leisure, an 'eat only the things you like' approach to diet and a childhood spent sedentary in front of computer and television screens indoors instead of energetically mobile in the fresh air. If we want the forces of a ruthless dictatorship to make mincemeat of our boys and to enslave what might be then left of our country, this is the way to go about it.

It is neither consolation nor excuse to remember that other western countries are no better. Danger comes from outside the circle of the soft.

THE NEAR AND MIDDLE EAST

As the junction of the three continents of Europe, Asia and Africa, the Near East has been of strategic importance since antiquity. Both by land or sea, trade routes have always led through this thinly populated region. Trade has naturally drawn war in its wake, giving military value to the Near East at an early date. The addition of two further factors to this vital geographical location has intensified the critical nature of the region in the present day: the possession of immense resources of oil and the rebirth of militant Islam.

With only three per cent of the world's population, the states of the Near and Middle East were responsible for forty per cent of worldwide arms purchases during the 1980s. Astonishingly, these countries together managed at times to spend more than twice as much on arms as the NATO and Warsaw Pact countries combined!

In the Near East, people are arming for wars of differing characters: for war on Israel, whose right to exist is still contested by many Arab states; for a 'classic' war against a neighbour, such as that between Iraq and Iran over hegemony on the Persian Gulf; and for a possible holy war *(Jihad)* of Muslims against western industrial nations – this last perhaps including a war of terrorism.

Israel is compelled to spend some thirty per cent of her gross national product annually on defence. Her citizens rightly regard their country as a democracy under fire. It is impossible to imagine the Israelis ever abandoning the possibilities of defence offered by atomic weapons. They live closer to reality than do we.

Three days after the Israeli state was founded in May 1948, it was attacked by the armies of no fewer than five Arab countries who loudly proclaimed their objective of taking the territory for the Arabs. The question of a journalist, what area was foreseen for Israeli settlement after an Arab victory, was answered by the Palestinian leader of those days with the assertion that such considerations were superfluous, since after the campaign there would be no more Israelis. As is well known, this still unresolved problem originated in the *diaspora*, or dispersal of the Jews, which followed the crushing by Roman legions in 135AD of a bitterly fought Jewish revolt. During the eighteen centuries which followed, Romans, Byzantines, Persians, Crusaders, Arabs and Turks succeeded one another as rulers of Palestine. With the dissolution of the Ottoman Empire at the end of the First World War, 400 years of Turkish rule over Palestine were at an end, though many Arabs remained settled there. Muslims had meanwhile erected their own Mosque of Omar on the site of the Jewish Temple which had been destroyed by the Romans. This spot remains a holy place for the adherents of both religions.

When the British relinquished their mandate over the territory in 1948, Palestine was divided. Their homeland was restored to the Jewish people by the founding of Israel. Jordan, with fewer inhabitants than Israel but almost five times the amount of land, offered the Palestine Arabs a home and citizenship. The Palestinians declined the offer. This is the root of the whole senseless tragedy of the continuing confrontations over the tiny state of Israel, which finds itself surrounded by no fewer than twenty-two Arab countries. The Palestinians have had a half-century and more in which to accept with thanks the offer of their Arab brothers, roll up their sleeves and set about building up a land to compare with Israel. Instead, the Palestinians have preferred to spend those more than fifty years lamenting their lot and retailing to a credulous world the propaganda of having no homeland, while waiting for a chance to destroy the Jewish state. There are some 90,000 firearms distributed among the Palestinians, many of whom are eager to send their own children forward to be killed as 'martyrs' for the national cause.

There will be no end to this murderous situation so long as the Palestinians continue to refuse to settle down in new homes among their Arab brethren. Finally to take this step would show vision on the part of Palestinians and place the Israelis under a moral obligation. Leaving aside the question whether any genuine desire to live at peace even exists at all, it is apparent that peoples with militantly conflicting racial loyalties and religious faiths cannot be expected to live together harmoniously in a single state. All talk of peace is meaningless so long as the two peoples are not separated by physical distance. The Palestinians need to be out of Israel altogether, in an Arab state – though it is essential that, as Muslims, they should be guaranteed access to their mosque in Jerusalem. At the same time, it would not be too much to ask Israel – with the help of Jews worldwide – to grant assistance to the Palestinians in building up their new homeland. So long as positive steps are not taken in this direction, murder will remain part of daily life.

Officially, Israel and Jordan have ended their war against one another. Even so, shortage of water, that perpetual bane of the Near and Middle East, could yet supply the *casus belli* for renewed hostilities between these two. Each nation uses more water than nature provides on its territory. It is in the interests of the outside world to give any help necessary in solving this problem.

Defending a compact territory demands a high degree of swiftness in reaction to attack. From Syria or Jordan, Israel can be traversed by car as far as the Mediterranean coast in an hour; an enemy aircraft can cross Israel in three minutes. The Israeli Air Force therefore occupies a key position in deterrence and defence planning. The American Patriot ABM system was supplied to Israel successfully during the Gulf War. Israel and the USA are now jointly developing the improved Arrow ABM system. The export of such weapons of defence has the disadvantage that they can be converted into offensive systems, though in the Near and Middle East only Israel is currently capable of doing this. France, which supplies many Arab countries, is developing her own ABM system, named Asta. Every ABM defence can of course be overrun, and it must be assumed that states such as Iraq, Syria and Iran are presently occupied with acquiring the latest generation of missiles. Iran has already secured the assistance of North Korean specialists in this field.

Best-armed among the Muslim states is Iraq, having the world's fourth largest army after those of Russia, China and the USA, as well as more warplanes and main battle tanks than Britain and France combined. Though Iraq's GNP is only one twentieth that of France, the Iraqis nonetheless have four times as many tanks and one and a half times as many warplanes as the French. With fifty per cent of Iraq's population consisting of Shiites, western experts fear that the possible overthrow of Saddam Hussein would be followed by the creation of a fundamentalist régime along the Iranian pattern, posing a danger to the outside world. Such fears may well be exaggerated; any revolts against Saddam's rule are perhaps more likely to be of social and political character, rather than religious.

Since the hatred between Iraq and Iran has been in existence since 637 AD (!), any hopes of an early reconciliation must be regarded as illusory. The roots of this persistent hostility lie even further back: in the fight between Arabs and Persians in antiquity over the rivers Tigris and Euphrates.

The twenty million or so Kurds distributed between Turkey, Armenia, Iran, Iraq and Syria are victims of a twentieth century omission. When the Turkish Empire was dissolved in the peace treaties of 1919, there was an opportunity to put the much-trumpeted idea of the self-determination of nations into practice by creating a Kurdistan. This was not done. By the terms of the cease-fire after the Gulf War, those Kurds living in Iraq north of the 36th Parallel were placed under the protection of the United Nations. Ignoring this, Iraqi troops attacked these Kurds at the end of August 1996 both from the air and with tanks. This blatant challenge to the West and to the UN went unpunished.

After the experiences of the short-lived occupation of Kuwait, western industrial countries have reduced their export of weapons to the Near and Middle East. The only missiles now supplied are those with the shortest range. On the other hand, it must be assumed that Russia, China, North Korea and possibly also the Czech Republic will continue their arms supplies to the states of this region. India and Brazil also seem unlikely to stand aside from possible business opportunities. India, in particular, striving for domination over all southern Asia, will be eager to earn desperately needed income through weapons sales.

After eight years of war against Iran, Iraq finally emerged as the victor once Iran no longer possessed any combat-ready air force.

Since the Iranian forces were equipped with American aircraft, the USA was able to bring about this situation through the simple expedient of an effective embargo on the export of spare parts.

All wars in the Near and Middle East have until now been fought with 'conventional', that is, non-nuclear weapons. After the Gulf War, UN observers reported that they had found twenty-six pounds of weapons-grade uranium in Iraq: seventeen pounds securely packed, the remaining nine pounds under rubble.

CHINA

When Portugal granted independence to her other colonies in 1975, the Chinese government announced that it was looking for no change in the status of Macao, Portugal's possession off the South China coast. In Portuguese hands for 400 years, Macao enjoyed the full autonomy of an overseas province of the Iberian state. Then the return of Hong Kong to China after expiry of Britain's 150-year lease loosed off a wave of chauvinism among the Chinese people.

Beijing soon demanded the return of Macao after all, this being implemented towards the end of 1999. The general talk is that Taiwan comes next. The Chinese government regards Taiwan as a renegade province. Western countries must make up their minds whether they wish to defend Taiwan's independence or whether they are prepared to watch her annexation by China with no more than token condemnation or even a shrug of the shoulders. Any realistic view of the situation indicates that the West will make no attempt to prevent the invasion and occupation of Taiwan. Inwardly, the West has almost certainly already written off Taiwan; the Beijing government will presumably be able select the date for annexation as it pleases.

Living in the atomic age can be intimidating. People are understandably reluctant to try to stop a nuclear-armed power in its tracks. All the same, the western world will be confronted with this question sooner or later. It would be wise to form a clear idea in advance of what to do *vis-à-vis* a China running amok, and to make the necessary military preparations well beforehand.

China for her part would do well to make any projected moves before the West – that is, America – has in place an effective system of defence against nuclear missiles. A rapid expansion of her submarine fleet and strategic missile arsenal would put China in a position to annex Taiwan while inflicting severe losses on America's Pacific seaboard should the USA act to interfere. Any tit for tat nuclear exchanges would clearly end in China's favour, since America would sensibly not persist in inviting losses in her homeland when that homeland itself was not the subject of any dispute. Should China delay in acting, then the US might later, with an SDI shield deployed, be able to fend off missile assaults while making China pay a heavy price for her aggression. Sooner, rather than later, would be in Beijing's interests. Remove nuclear weapons from the equation, of course, and China has nothing at all to fear, either now or later.

It is abundantly clear that China will play the determining role of pacesetter in world events of the twenty-first century. Russia, suffering severely from a setback to her self-confidence, will try to find her way back to a leading position in the world by teaming up with her stronger neighbour. In the long run, though, China will have absolutely no need of Russia. Beijing can indulge Moscow with co-operation for a limited period, as long as there are possible advantages such as technological assistance to be gained. Thereafter, China will be able to drop the Russians without a qualm, and be able to make her own way alone. China is the proverbial sleeping giant, and this giant is in the process of waking. In the coming decades, China will play the same sort of role on the world stage as was played by Germany in the twentieth century.

China faces the new century with a population already numbering 1,200 millions. In the next decades, the volume of her economy will overtake that of the United States. This will make China not only the most populous nation on earth, but the richest as well.

Hopes of democratization in China may prove to be less well founded than similar hopes for Russia. Where is there a place for criticism and opposition in a country whose journalists actually take pride in the fact that the world's first newspaper was founded in China as a means for the emperor to tell the people what he expected of them? The Chinese mind still sees the role of the press as communicating the edicts and propaganda of the country's rulers.

In due course, the population of China will burst the physical boundaries of the country. The most likely eventuality then is that China's hand will reach out towards the fertile lands of southern Asia. The endless Chinese hordes may well stream into countries from West Pakistan to Singapore, exterminating the native population, to settle the lands themselves. It was once the Chinese who were themselves victims, not perpetrators, of such a policy. In the early thirteenth century, the Mongols killed an estimated forty million people in clearing northern China of her inhabitants to create the land we know as Mongolia. For seven centuries, this remained the largest act of genocide in history, until Soviet Russia set a new world record. Now the pressure is in the opposite direction. A significant proportion of China's surplus population may well spill over her boundaries to the west and north, into Russia's eastern territories. The border between Russia and China runs for almost 5,000 miles – the world's longest land frontier. The rivers Amur and Ussuri form part of these boundaries. Both countries claim the Ussuri, but have agreed that the border should run along the middle of the river. Whether the Chinese search for living space will also extend towards Japan is something which only time will reveal.

China has accurate missiles, but her most significant resource lies in her enormous human reserves. These will allow China to survive nuclear assault while herself continuing to pour men into the attack. In the world's most populous country, human losses take on a dimension utterly different from European standards. Sixty million dead would make a desert of Britain; for China they might mean only some welcome relief from overcrowding. According to an old Chinese proverb, military sacrifices are not particularly highly valued: *'Good iron is not used for nails; good men are not used as soldiers'*. Despite this, it must be acknowledged that China's present armed forces have largely replaced quantity with quality. The Asian giant's best units are trained to the highest standards, even the newest recruits demonstrating a discipline such as has rarely been seen in the West since 1945. These forces will soon have in their hands weapons reflecting the pinnacle of current technology.

THE PACIFIC

North Korea, which possesses the world's fifth largest army, has until now resisted all diplomatic attempts to have her nuclear research centres inspected by the International Atomic Energy Agency. The communist government claims to be engaging in nuclear research only for peaceful purposes, but western experts have concluded that North Korea has already developed her own atomic weapons.

During the 1960s, the Soviets built a nuclear research centre with a five-megawatt reactor on the Kunon River, only some sixty or so miles from the North Korean capital Pyongyang. Since then, 25-megawatt and 250-megawatt reactors have been added. Uranium is mined in North Korea itself and converted into plutonium by beta-decay. Between three and six kilograms of plutonium are required to build a nuclear weapon. Facilities for converting uranium into plutonium are of course unnecessary for electricity generation.

If the installations on the Kunon were really built to provide electrical power, they would be connected to the national grid, which is not the case.

Significantly, North Korea abandoned its adherence to the Nuclear Non-Proliferation Treaty in March 1993 – a step which unleashed fears that South Korea, Japan and Taiwan could feel obliged also to build their own nuclear weapons.

During the 1990s, air defences round Pyongyang were considerably strengthened, in particular by the deployment of ground-to-air missiles.

In December 1992, the North Korean government announced its intention of reuniting Korea, using force if necessary, by 1995. This would have meant a revival of the failed attempt started by Pyongyang in 1950. To emphasize the threat, 800,000 North Korean soldiers with tanks and artillery were deployed along the border with the demilitarized zone which runs between North and South. Multiple rocket launchers were transferred to sites close to the frontier, battle training was intensified and ammunition depots replenished. Nothing further happened, but in the autumn of 1993, the USA felt compelled to make preparations for a cruise missile attack on the installations on the Kunon.

Experts consider the North Korean régime to be the world's most ruthless tyranny. Following the example of other communist states, North Korea is now attempting to give her dictatorship an appearance of democracy. Both the USA and Japan are making discreet diplomatic efforts to wean North Korea away from her unbending ideological behaviour by means of generous financial assistance. Naturally, such a course can easily go wrong; monetary aid can be used as much to build up armaments as to create alternatives to them. The Pyongyang régime has urgent need of financial relief; in 1990 it spent forty per cent of its budget on its armed forces, while between 1990 and 1992 GNP fell by more than fifteen per cent. In addition, North Korea suffers from a shortage of foodstuffs. China supplies the major part of her requirements in oil, coal and grain, and the Beijing government's attitude is likely to be decisive for North Korea's future.

Western industrial states will not remain unaffected, and might well be drawn in to some extent, by any conflicts involving China and North Korea on the one side and, say, South Korea and Japan on the other. The Pacific region is rich in further tensions capable of erupting into purely regional warfare, from which western powers are likely to be determined to remain aloof. War between Vietnam and Cambodia, for example, is not only possible but probable.

Singapore could be attacked by an envious Muslim Malaysia. Singapore enjoys close ties to the West, and is building up her own arms industry, much of it in very advanced fields, including missiles. Like Kuwait, Singapore is a rich country with envious, hostile neighbours.

Singapore, with fewer than three million inhabitants, possesses the world's busiest harbour, where there are never fewer than seven hundred ships at any one time. Sensibly, Singapore is building a navy. After having been occupied by the Japanese in 1942, the people of Singapore are only too aware of their vulnerability, fearing potential threats from the navies of neighbouring states –

those of India, Pakistan, Indonesia, Malaysia, Vietnam and China. Offsetting such threats, the West has treaty obligations towards Singapore, as well as close and important economic and industrial ties with her.

Malaysia's possible expansionist dreams may be assumed from an appeal by her Prime Minister to expand her population from the present eighteen millions to seventy millions by the end of the twenty-first century. Malaysian couples are urged to have at least three children – this in an age when an 'explosion' of population constitutes the gravest world problem of all. Officially, this campaign is justified with the complaint that there is a shortage of workers in Malaysia.

In response, a worried Singapore has decided likewise to encourage an increased birth rate.

Significant Chinese minorities live in Singapore, Malaysia, Indonesia and the Philippines, where they form the heart of the business communities. Without the skills of the Chinese, the economies of these states would be significantly weaker.

The Chinese minority fell victim to what looked like organized mobs in Indonesia during riots in 1998. Hundreds of Chinese were murdered and thousands lost their livelihoods when their business premises were burned down. Chinese women and even young girls were raped repeatedly by gangs which broke into their homes.

The troubles had started with an attempt (eventually successful) to topple the Indonesian dictator Suharto. Chinese living in Indonesia became incidental victims, financial envy being an obvious motivation.

So far, the Chinese government has shown no sign of concern over such events. All the same, these Chinese minorities in the states of Southeast Asia and the Pacific could one day provide Beijing with a welcome excuse to invade, in order to protect their fellow-countrymen.

Racial minorities in other Pacific states, among them Indians in Fiji and the Solomon Islands, have been victims of similar violence. Resentment caused by immigrants, when these become too numerous and appear to be taking over their adopted home, is an obvious recipe for civil wars which might well draw in other states.

It is chiefly in the minds of educated people of European stock that resentment of immigrants is felt to be wrong. Their view is not shared by the overwhelming majority of the world's population. To ignore the powerful factor of national feelings is to deny reality.

Sadly, experience shows us that of all man's attributes, his capacity for failing to learn from observation is one of the most remarkable.

The governments of Australia and New Zealand displayed their own particular lack of contact with reality when they declared their countries to be 'nuclear-free zones'. Like neutrality, the question whether a country remains 'nuclear-free' is decided not by its own government but by the governments of other countries. One might equally well declare one's house to be a 'rain-free area' and remove the roof. How the peoples of Australia and New Zealand – rich, fertile but sparsely inhabited countries – imagine that they are going to defend themselves should the proverbial balloon go up, is beyond imagination. They will not be able to do so alone. Without the West, they will be hopelessly lost – and how will the West be able to help them without using nuclear weapons?

In the face of China's rapidly advancing technology, it is in any case an open question how long the West's nuclear-armed submarines will be able to continue patrolling the Pacific undetected.

AFRICA

During the last thirty years of the twentieth century alone, wars and civil wars in Africa cost more than seven million human lives. Of the world's forty-four million refugees, half are Africans.

At the time when the Gold Coast received her independence from Britain in 1957, her population was enjoying a GNP per capita on the same level as that of South Korea. During forty years of native self-government, the former colony, now known as Ghana, has suffered continual decline in her standard of living, and is now one of the world's poorest countries. During the same period, the South Koreans have worked their way up to a position among the richer nations; South Korea now enjoys a GNP per capita sixteen times (!) that of Ghana.

These contrasting performances highlight the catastrophic picture applying to most former colonies of European powers. Two thirds of the world's poorest states are to be found in Africa, with the foreign debts of most countries south of the Sahara greater than their annual national incomes.

Nonetheless, their governments always have money for weapons.

In this most grievously overpopulated continent, there is never any shortage of causes for bloody strife.

Civil wars which followed the attainment of independence by the former Portuguese colony of Angola (annual income per capita ca. 500 US dollars) cost more than 200,000 killed, with a further half million dying of starvation. There are estimated to be anything up to twenty million mines still in the ground in Angola, which unsurprisingly is said to have more amputees than any other country in the world. Damage to Angola's infrastructure is on no less horrifying a scale. According to the United Nations, fighting in Angola caused destruction amounting to seventeen billion US dollars, while in addition eighty per cent of the country's agricultural land was made unusable. Angola's railways had been built by Scots engineers; during the fighting, 385 of the network's 390 bridges were destroyed.

It was no surprise, though long overdue, when BBC Radio's World Service broadcast a report from Angola in the early hours of December 26, 1999, in which black Angolans were heard regretting the end of Portuguese rule over their country. The Portuguese, said the participants, had looked after the natives; since independence, on the other hand, their own people had brought them nothing but war and bloodshed.

Ethnic (tribal) differences are just as much a danger to African peace as hunger, envy and greed. Colonial territories were created in accordance with the claims and rivalries of the European ruling powers. The result was an arbitrary drawing-up of frontiers without regard to the composition of the native population within those boundaries. Ancient incompatibilities and straightforward hatred among the diverse peoples were simply ignored by the colonial rulers. The price was paid once the territories became independent.

Nigeria, for example, was created through colonization by the British of the territories of no fewer than 250 different tribes. In 1967, the Ibos, a largely Christian people in the south of Nigeria, attempted to achieve independence of their own by founding a new state, to be named Biafra. The suppression of these efforts, through the massive physical superiority of other tribes, cost more than a million lives during the next three years of ruthless civil war, in which a principal role was played by Muslim Hausas from the north of the country.

Just as in the creation of Yugoslavia and Czechoslovakia by the victorious powers in 1919, so too in the overseas colonies none of the peoples concerned was asked whether it wished to be included in the same agglomeration as another. From Biafra to Rwanda, the consequences have been an endless succession of massacres. Four hundred years of hatred between Hutus and Tutsis have erupted in the bloodiest possible fashion in both Rwanda and neighbouring Burundi, which until 1919 had been parts of German East Africa.

Wars of extermination between various native peoples, as in the case of the Hutus and the Tutsis, are likely to be everyday affairs in twenty-first century Africa.

One significant factor was added during the years of colonial rule, unwittingly to act as an aggravation of ancient enmities: the discovery of mineral riches for which earlier there was no use and which are now in continual demand by the industrial nations. Oil for the world's motors and copper for the wires and contacts essential to every electrical appliance are vital components of the African economy, as too are diamonds and gold.

That the self-governing African states remain poor despite these riches does little to encourage confidence in the continent's future. What is certain is that unexpected possession of massive assets – and they include minerals such as nickel, manganese and even uranium – can only increase the frequency of bloodshed in Africa.

Wars are practically unavoidable between:

Nigeria and her neighbour Cameroon over oil rights (oil accounts for ninety-five per cent of Nigeria's export trade);

Somalia and Kenya over a border dispute;

Eritrea and Ethiopia, similarly in a boundary question;

Ethiopia and Somalia, also over border territories.

In Africa, the contrasts between the richest and the poorest countries are particularly crass, almost inviting attack.

The entire continent is one gigantic disaster area, from north to south and from east to west. The situation will not be helped by the rapid multiplication of Nigerians. By 2035, the population of Nigeria is expected to have overtaken those of both the United States and Russia, making the heavily indebted African republic the third most populous country on earth after China and India.

THE THIRD WORLD

Strictly speaking, the 'Third World' comprises not just the poor, underdeveloped countries, but block-free states as well. Many of these are stable and thriving, and represent no threat to peace.

Material differences between the most prosperous and the impoverished countries are now greater than they have been at any time previously. The foreign debts of states in southern Asia, Latin America and the Caribbean are equivalent to almost forty per cent of their annual GNPs.

Despite rising debt levels, arms are being purchased with increased eagerness. In 1960, armed forces in what has come to be called the 'Third World' totalled 8.7 million men. By the middle of the 1980s, the number had already reached fifteen millions.

Young technicians from the Third World, trained in industrial countries, return in due course to their homelands, where they frequently work on weapons programmes of a nature worrying to the rest of us. Third World countries which cannot afford the most expensive armaments systems resort to the alternatives of chemical and sometimes biological weapons. These are considerably cheaper and promise a much higher casualty rate. The poor country's substitute for a nuclear weapon is the fuel-air bomb, which has five times the detonation power of conventional TNT, but is not considered in the West to be a significant weapon against the forces of an industrial nation.

Conditions in many countries cause one to shake one's head in bafflement. Brazil, for instance, which will become a rich industrial country in the near future, produces more steel than France and is already an exporter of arms as well as of coffee and tobacco. Despite this, Brazil remains a country of senseless contrasts: it is the world's fourth largest exporter of foodstuffs at the same time as occupying sixth place among those nations whose citizens are suffering from permanent undernourishment. A sizeable proportion of Brazil's population is going hungry, while comestibles are being sold to other countries. This is the sort of state with whose government the industrial nations must attempt somehow to deal.

At the same time, it would be appropriate for the industrial nations themselves to act a little more rationally and generously. Across the globe, some 40,000 human beings die of hunger every day. On every one of these days, the European Union spends more than £20 million on storing and/or destroying (!) surplus stocks of foodstuffs, chiefly beef, butter and grain.

While food is being consigned to wasteful incineration in Europe, hunger has become a permanent condition only a short flight away, in the Sudan. In this largest of all African countries (roughly the size of western Europe), life expectancy is forty-eight years.

There are an estimated 1,000 million people worldwide suffering from permanent hunger, while the USA produces an annual food surplus of one third (production equalling four thirds of domestic requirements). Even the giant, nuclear-armed poverty state of India has stores of surplus grain unconsumed because millions of Indians cannot afford to pay for this nourishment.

Among the 867-million-strong population of India are fourteen million Sikhs, whose aspirations to autonomy have already led to fighting and will undoubtedly produce further bloodshed. Renewed battles are similarly to be expected between Muslims and Hindus, while in neighbouring Sri Lanka the Tamil minority is fighting for an independent state in notably bloody fashion, including terrorism.

The outside world will be less affected by such wars than by, for instance, a renewed conflict between India and Pakistan for possession of Kashmir. Two thirds of Kashmir is part of the Indian republic, which also lays claim to the remainder, belonging to Pakistan. This remaining third is populated by Muslims, who wish to remain with their co-religionists as citizens of Pakistan. Open war has broken out three times between the two states over this matter, the last time in 1971.

India's aim is a Greater India including the territory of Pakistan. Indians see Muslim Pakistan as a foreign body on Indian soil, and wish to convert their Muslim cousins back to Hinduism. Radical

Hindus are no less fanatical than their Muslim neighbours, arguing that Hinduism must become *the* religion of the twenty-first century.

The fact that both states now possess nuclear weapons ought to deter them from a fourth Kashmir war, but the ever more militant attitudes developing on both sides appear to make effective deterrence unlikely. This is the part of the world where the first nuclear war may be expected.

Elsewhere, Muslim extremists are causing concern with their demand for a Muslim world state, which would occupy a belt of territory practically around the globe, stretching from Morocco to Indonesia. Any such development would quickly expose as a grave error the industrial nations' keenness to sell arms to Third World countries. Weapons sales to Iraq, a Third World state without any industrial base of her own, already allowed that country to blossom into a kind of regional superpower within a decade. Almost certainly, willingness to supply Iraq with weapons was fuelled by the wish to have a strong counterbalance to militant Islamic Iran. The outcome is that the world now finds itself facing an Iraq equipped with highly developed and unpleasant weapons systems. Iraq is capable, among other things, of arming her SCUD-B rockets with chemical warheads.

Normally, it is possible to cripple the armed forces of a client state. The computer technology necessary to keep the latest American warplanes flying, for instance, is a consumable article and available only from the US. An air force equipped with these machines can be grounded within days if not supplied with the necessary items.

One enormous problem in the Third World resides in the ca. 119 million anti-personnel mines which are lying in the earth of more than seventy states as a legacy of civil and international wars and still claiming victims among civilian populations. Anti-personnel mines cost something like £2.50 each; operations to clear them, on the other hand, average out at about £700 for every one. In countries which cannot afford heavy weapons, these small mines offer an inexpensive protection against approaching foot soldiers. There are estimated to be some ten million mines in Cambodia's soil, while even Europe is not entirely free of the problem: Bosnia is entering the twenty-first century with some six million mines literally underfoot.

The Third World has soldiers as young as seven years. These children are chiefly used in civil wars to guard prisoners, carry messages and so on, but are generally also forced to kill. Many youngsters join an armed unit to avenge the death of their parents; others are simply abducted by armed units and forced into service. Even girls are not exempt. The average age of soldiers killed in the wars of industrial nations is nineteen years. Even without reliable statistics, it is apparent that for the most part the dead of Third World battles are some years younger still.

Many Third World conflicts, both civil wars and warfare between states, have their origins in the over-hasty dissolution of colonial empires carried out during the 1950s and 1960s. The colonies of European powers were given independence without adequate time being devoted to the necessary induction of their peoples into a spirit of responsible and non-violent democracy

The tendency is self-evident among former colonial territories for the forms of equitable government bequeathed them by their former masters to become perverted over time into bloodthirsty one-party dictatorships. It starts with the use of armed gangs to beat and murder supporters of opposition groups in order to win 'democratic' elections through intimidation. It ends with wholesale slaughter and a régime which can be removed, if at all, only through armed force at the cost of countless lives. Anyone not realizing this has not been following the daily news.

Admittedly, our own democracy is full of flaws. It gives us governments whose election turns their heads with the conceit that they have been 'chosen' by the people. All but a few are both too dim and too vain to realize that they have won merely because the public wanted to be rid of their predecessors. Apparently deceiving even themselves, these 'democrats' practise the hypocrisy that they have a 'manifesto commitment' to introduce measures which the public not only does not want, but had not even anticipated. Politicians in government posture as though nobly honouring an obligation, while knowing full well that not one voter in a thousand has even seen their party manifesto, let alone read it. This is the sharp practice of the dubious salesman with his unreadable pale-grey tiny print on the reverse, unseen side of a contract.

Our politicians appear concerned only to indulge their own prejudices, that is, they concentrate on forcing or rushing through legislation gratifying the particular bees in their own bonnets, contemptuously thrusting aside those more material issues on which the public in general is crying out for action. This conduct they call 'democracy'. The saving grace is that, unlike the citizens of dictatorships, we can throw out our rulers after a few years. 'Con-men' are unpleasant and undesirable, but they cause humanity less pain and misery than do gangsters.

In the first weeks after Britain had relinquished her rule over the Indian subcontinent, establishing the independent republics of India and Pakistan, no fewer than 750,000 people were killed in civil disturbances and fifteen millions driven from their homes. For almost two hundred years, the British had kept order on a subcontinent whose inhabitants outnumbered the military and civilian members of the administration by well over a thousand to one. It will be apparent to all that such laughably small British forces could never have withstood any serious rising of the indigent population. Order was maintained by the force of moral strength. With independence, this order was abruptly no longer a factor.

A particularly crass example of failure to learn from example can be found in Haiti, which was a Spanish possession for two centuries after Columbus (until 1697). During the next hundred years, Haiti became France's richest colony. Independent from 1804, Haiti was administered by the US from 1915 to 1934. Despite the advantage of having enjoyed such talented teachers – Spanish, French and American – Haiti remains one of the most backward and poorest countries in the western hemisphere, indeed, in the entire world.

Many Haitian families have an income of only 100 US dollars per year. For every Haitian child in secondary education there are 189 members of the security forces. Never in the almost 300 years since Haiti became the first Caribbean colony to achieve independence

162

has she enjoyed democratic government. Haiti may represent no threat to world peace; all the same, she serves as a sharp reminder that developing nations do not necessarily share the humane values customary among the peoples of industrial states.

Peace-loving nations should never take their eyes off events in the Third World. A general rule of thumb is that the higher the proportion of illiteracy among a country's population, the keener its government's striving for military potency.

THE UNITED STATES

Since annexing Hawaii in 1898, America has been not just an Atlantic power but a Pacific one as well.

The course being followed by Washington is a continuation of the established foreign policy of graduated deterrence, alongside support for selected groups of freedom fighters opposing communism. This policy is determined by the State Department and the National Security Council. The aim is to preserve peace through strength.

It is probable that in time the United States will be crippled by the costs of acting as the world's policeman. Americans are certain to learn that worldwide actions and interventions are too expensive in the long run. The United States themselves will suffer, and Washington will eventually be forced to concentrate its efforts on defence of its home territory.

America might even withdraw into her former isolation without having overspent. For this, it will be enough for Washington simply to have the impression that her allies have let her down.

During the Gulf crisis of 1990, the USA asked other countries to contribute financially to the upkeep of American troops in Saudi Arabia (a matter of forty million dollars daily). Saudi Arabia herself pledged monthly contributions, while the exiled government of Kuwait similarly made a commitment. Japan and Germany also accepted their share of the burden. This is an indication of how difficult it has become for the USA to mount such operations, and it is a lesson which governments in Beijing and elsewhere will not have failed to note.

In 1990 the US government expected a budget deficit of 100 billion dollars and set itself the target of reducing this shortage to sixty-four billions in 1991. Despite an election promise *('Watch my lips')* not to increase taxes, President Bush was obliged to raise them after all, because of the fiscal deficit. In the event, matters were much worse than had been anticipated: the true amount of deficit in 1990 proved to be 230 billions, and in 1991 it rose to 350 billions. By 1998 the deficit had shot up to 550 billions. Despite these deficiencies, an overwhelming majority of American citizens pronounced themselves at the end of 1998 satisfied with Clinton's presidency 'because we are doing so well financially' – an alarming insight into the capacity for judgement of a democratic and on the whole well-educated public.

With or without good sense on the part of the people, real circumstances will still have an impact on military policy, and it is facts which one has to consider, not the pronouncements of an electorate.

During the 1950s, the USA was able to put 3,000 new military aircraft into service every year, scrapping those being replaced. By 1990, annual procurement had shrunk to 150 new machines. The fact is that the sophisticated development of all weapons – whether tanks, aircraft, artillery pieces, warships or simple infantry arms – has driven their prices to horrendously high levels. Even an infantryman's rifle is not to be compared with its simpler predecessor from the Second World War. Where heavy weapons are concerned, the staggering costs are attributable in part to electronic components and modern materials.

Sensibly, America's nuclear deterrent is a structure supported on three legs: missiles which can be fired from the underground silos in which they are stored, those on board submarines and others carried by long-range bombers.

Active defence is offered by strategic rockets which can destroy an enemy's missiles in their silos. Passive defence comes from anti-ballistic missile systems. Where these latter are concerned, it has to be conceded that they are vulnerable to decoy missiles and to interference via radar. They can also simply be overwhelmed by the simultaneous assault of great numbers of offensive weapons.

In all these technical areas, above all in that of electronic guidance systems, America is well ahead of any potential opponent. On land, at sea and in the air, as also in space, American weapons and equipment are the very best that there is. In the immediate future, the Pentagon's planning staffs need fear no rivals. Backing up America's gigantic technical lead is her massive production potential, which already proved to be decisive in the great wars of the twentieth century.

Where America's armed forces themselves are concerned, reliance on electronics, with its wishful thinking of 'hands off' wars, have resulted in many officers becoming more like industrial managers than fighting men. In time, this trend is likely to be followed by the forces of other countries. Fundamentally, this is a natural development more or less imposed by advances in technology.

Cause for anxiety is contained in a report by a former Chief of the US Army's General Staff, General Edward C. Meyer. According to Meyer's assessment, the American Army at the turn of the century is no longer fit for combat. Meyer complained of inadequacies in air and sea transport facilities, as well as in systems for support and supply of the fighting troops in any theatre of war.

As an example, Meyer pointed to lack of communications channels between command centres in the USA and forces on the ground during the 1983 invasion of Grenada. He quoted the case of an American officer who was able to discuss the situation on the ground with his superiors back home only by using his own personal credit card to telephone his wife with the request that she connect him with his headquarters.

As Meyer stressed, any such inadequacies in US conventional forces could easily make it necessary to go over to the use of nuclear weapons earlier than anticipated.

In a non-nuclear world, America's prospects would appear to be less assured, unless – as is quite feasible – laser weapons for both strategic and battlefield use can be produced and deployed in sufficient numbers. Whatever America does, the world will not stand still. Laser weapon countermeasures will one day be in the hands of opponents.

Any suggestions?

THE UNITED NATIONS

Ideally, the government of every country should know that as a member of the United Nations it is in the same position as any individual citizen within his own society – namely, that it must adhere to the laws of the community or suffer punishment. A member country would be acknowledging this legal situation by the act of joining the UN. Any state not a member would be regarded as remaining outside the international community, that is, would be more or less an outlaw. Terminating one's membership in the UN would not and should not confer freedom of action.

None of this should be taken as a plea for world government. Every nation should manage its own affairs without interference from others – provided that it respects at least a minimum standard of human rights. The United Nations should be in effect a family of self-governing peoples. Never should UNO attempt to act as one unified government. All the same, the use of force by one state against another should as far as is practical not go unpunished.

It may be wonderfully convenient for some peoples to avoid the sacrifices and hardships of war and to live on unmolested themselves, thanks to the actions of those other nations who *are* prepared to step in to help others. This can never be a permanent situation, since any country acting as the world's peacemaker will eventually fight itself into bankruptcy.

In 1938, the last full year of peace before the Second World War, Britain's total fiscal budget required 12.5 per cent of national income. By 1943, at the high point of the war, the proportion had shot up to fifty-two per cent. We need not be surprised at the consequences.

Since the Second World War, their sophisticated technological development has made so-called 'conventional', that is, non-nuclear weapons, so expensive that the costs of even smaller wars can seriously threaten the economic survival of most states. Even after taking into consideration the fall in the value of money since 1939 (the pound is now worth one twenty-fifth of its value then), a present-day RAF fighter costs two hundred times as much as its predecessors, the Hurricane and Spitfire. Inflation on much the same scale applies also to tanks, artillery pieces and other heavy weapons, warships and even basic infantry arms. Yet no state on earth is two hundred times richer than it was in 1939; on the contrary, many of the belligerent nations of those days have meanwhile become significantly poorer.

Recorded history shows that every great power ultimately collapses economically because of the cost of the warfare which repeatedly becomes necessary to re-establish and maintain peace.

And the United Nations?

What strengths does UNO possess to deal with countries which break the peace?

Which criminal dictatorships tremble at the thought of UN intervention?

What is there about UNO to convince potential aggressors that it combines military potency with implacable will?

Relationships between states, unlike those between individual citizens within a state, are not regulated by any established system of law and order. If UNO is really to be effective and actually to fulfil those tasks of restoring and maintaining peace with which her founders entrusted her, a radical change in the thinking and conduct of most member states will first be necessary.

His neighbours do not – one hopes – simply stand by and watch while a householder repeatedly torments, mistreats and even murders members of his family. They step in, call for police to enter the house, put an end to the evil and save the victims from further suffering. As long as the world community fails to take the same sort of action towards violent nations, there will be no progress in minimizing the frequency and scope of war. Just as police are empowered to enter and search households, UN forces must be entitled to cross frontiers at any time to put an end to violence and abuses of human rights. This would mean abandoning the concept of absolute sovereignty within one's own borders – a notion of immunity which ought now, but is unlikely to be, considered obsolete. Intervention in wars between states in order to end them –

this was the twentieth century's great step forward. If mankind wants to advance any further towards the objective of keeping to a minimum the suffering caused by war, it must also be prepared to intervene in civil wars as well, whenever humanitarian disasters make this necessary. Theoretically, anyway.

No one, of course, will intervene in the most powerful countries. Russia, for example, need have no fear of foreign armies coming in to stop her mistreatment of minorities striving for independence, no matter how ruthlessly she acts. Recognizing this fact is an acknowledgement that there will never be absolute equality between peoples and states where peacekeeping is concerned. Weaker nations will always be disciplined by the stronger, while the strong will tend to remain above the law.

Essentials for any use of UN forces are unity, determination and clarity: unity and determination on the part of nations providing the forces, and absolute clarity about the nature of the task. Instead, there are repeated situations like that involving the Albanian minority in the Serbian province of Kosovo during the 1990s. Members of this minority people, including children, were shot by Serbian snipers as soon as they left their homes. Many of their houses were burned down to drive them out like grouse for shooting. A great number, including babies, the old and the infirm, fled into the woods, where they were safe from sniper fire, to live for months like Stone Age people with primitive food supplies and in constant fear of death. UN troops who were only a mile or two away did nothing to protect these poor people.

The snipers could have been eliminated quickly – but UNO had not issued its forces with any mandate to do this. It was months before the United Nations took any notice of the situation. It then acted with a terrifying decisiveness calculated to curdle the blood of every Serbian murderer: it passed a resolution condemning the crimes.

Whether to intervene at all to save lives was a decision left by the United Nations to NATO ministers. Such a situation is not merely a farce; it is a disgrace and a crime in itself. According to their mandate, UN forces were simply to show their teeth to the Serbs;

their very presence was expected to intimidate. Yet it is a crime to watch atrocities without acting. This only confers equal guilt.

Attempts were made to excuse this spineless failure by differentiating between peacemaking (active intervention to put an end to hostilities) and peacekeeping (supervision to prevent a renewed outbreak of fighting). Semantic gymnastics of this kind are totally irrelevant in such situations, as is hiding behind the terms of inadequate mandates. It is not just in failing to act, either to make or to keep the peace, that UNO displays lack of essential determination. Even in carrying out straightforward humanitarian tasks, the outstanding characteristic of the United Nations is lack of moral fibre. In newly independent states of the former Yugoslavia, UN troops *asked* the Serbs who were besieging a starving civilian population for *permission* (!) to take food and urgently needed medicines to the suffering people. It should be noted that these were no female aid workers doing the begging, but young, fit, fully-trained fighting men – organized forces armed with the most modern weapons and equipment from the richest countries on earth. Yet because UNO had given them no mandate to act, they were obliged to stand by and watch the destruction of a helpless civilian population.

A 'peace' mission of which UNO's member states can be truly proud!

'Peacekeeping' forces, of whom one is entitled to expect that they will at least try to keep the extent of human suffering to a minimum, have only one way to act in such situations: they give notice, first, that an aid convoy *will* be driven into the besieged area, and, second, that any attempt to stop it will be met with destructive fire. It is, after all, soldiers whom one has on the ground, not milkmaids.

Before any troops are despatched, there must be unequivocal understanding of the terms of their mission. It goes without saying that troop strength and weapons must be commensurate with the demands likely to be made on them. Above all, no country should agree to provide troops for UN missions without complete understanding that these forces will be used in any way necessary to

171

deal with all situations arising. Looking on like goggle-eyed tourists neither creates nor keeps the peace.

All decisions when and where to intervene, and to what extent, must be entirely a matter for the judgement of military commanders on the ground. Nonetheless, the overall commander should be assigned a political representative of UNO with whom decisions on actions likely to have political effects can be made jointly.

Intervention where there are murders or other war crimes, as in Kosovo, requires no discussion. Action to prevent or terminate such incidents fulfils a humanitarian necessity, a policing task. There is need for neither justification nor explanation. The simple fact that UN troops are present must be mandate enough to stop any murders without discussion or reference back, and without hesitation. Any such action has to be regarded as an automatic component of any UN mission and not to be rescinded. It is unthinkable that UNO representatives, of all people, should ever fail to carry out a simple humanitarian duty. Entry into the fighting, whether an internal conflict or a war between states, is on the other hand a political step, even when prompted by humanitarian considerations.

Only a man on the ground can make effective decisions. Referring questions back to meetings at UN headquarters can only slow down necessary action to the point of being self-defeating. UNO's political representative in the field must be someone with a proven dedication to decisive action, not the familiar wishy-washy talker too timid either to act or to react.

One lesson from the events of the twentieth century which is unmistakably clear for all to see is that eventually a point is reached at which the talking has to stop, giving way to action. There should be no place in international affairs for anyone who has not grasped this most fundamental of lessons, or who is incapable of recognizing the critical juncture when it is reached.

UN personnel simply pulled out of Angola early in 1999, when the situation in that country's long-running civil war became alarming. In the former Yugoslavia, the UN's mandate was repeatedly widened, without strengthening either the numbers of troops deployed or the arms at their disposal. Forces were despatched to the Balkans without heavy artillery, leaving them incapable of decisive intervention in any fighting. Deploying forces like this is totally pointless and a consequence of the spineless mentality which UNO will have to shed if it is not to die the same death as its predecessor, the League of Nations.

A more realistic way of thinking would necessarily ensure that with every UN mission the national character of the peoples concerned would be taken fully into account. For the troops who are sent in, this is at least as important as considerations of terrain and weather. Not every people fights with the same methods as the advanced industrial nations, not every one has the same values or is subject to the same moral inhibitions. Not every government has signed the Geneva Conventions or the Hague Treaties, and not every one – including some countries which are signatories – adheres to these rules.

UNO is a very long way from having demonstrated any sense of realism, let alone determination and united action. After the experience of Iraq's occupation of Kuwait, when it was not the UN General Secretary but representatives of the United States who were left to make diplomatic efforts to solve the crisis without war, it is hardly surprising that independent action is being taken more and more often, without reference to UNO.

In the few cases where UNO manages to pull itself together sufficiently to make some sort of a decision to act, it is then always the same nations which provide servicemen for the task. As time goes by, we can perceive the emergence of a 'coalition of the willing', as it is coming to be called. These willing nations are to be found chiefly among the member states of NATO. The first to volunteer their forces are always the British and Americans. This readiness on their part reflects the realistic attitude which both countries have developed through their involvement on the world stage, as well as their sense of responsibility towards their fellow-humans. Awareness of humanitarian obligation is a part of the national character of both peoples.

In this connection, it is noticeable that those other countries whose leaders always condemn the unilateral military actions of the British and Americans have themselves *never* in their history lifted a hand to do anything for anyone else, all their wars having been fought exclusively in furtherance or in defence of their own interests. As an example, one need think only of Russia. Such peoples, who have proven that they would never help anyone else in their times of need, are not entitled to express any opinion on other nations' efforts to bring about or to keep the peace.

Even among many countries which have actually provided troops for Blue Helmet missions, there has been a noticeable reluctance to suffer casualties. When the situation has worsened, these troop contingents have not been reinforced, but withdrawn. There are only certain indomitable nations which can be counted on to take risks for the freedom of others.

If there is no drastic change of attitude at the United Nations, the question of the UN's establishing its own peacekeeping force will simply disappear. What should actually be the function of the UN will be left permanently to the governments of individual states. The fact is that in any case the professional forces of leading NATO states do the job better than any troops from other countries. Thanks to their superior training, leadership, equipment and discipline, they bring off difficult tasks faster and at less human and material cost.

When UNO was founded, it was assumed (at least by Winston Churchill, who had had the same expectation of the League of Nations after the First World War) that the organization would set up its own permanent armed forces. Very probably because of mutual distrust during the 'Cold War', nothing came of this. With the collapse of the Soviet Union, UNO has an opportunity greater than before. Now would be the time to undertake those first steps which would justify the existence of the UN.

Permanent UN forces must be armed and trained for every type of warfare, including guerrilla fighting, on every continent, on every type of terrain and in every climate.

How little UNO actually does towards making peace out of war, and then keeping the peace, can be recognized from the fact that in a typical year the total costs of Blue Helmet missions are less than the amount spent annually by the City of New York alone, for police and fire brigade.

UNO has other roles to fulfil besides that of peacekeeping. These were brought about by problems arising from the outcome of the Second World War: aid for refugees, countering hunger, health care and the creation of educational and cultural systems in developing countries. Without doubt a great deal has been achieved in these fields, yet unity in despatching UN troops to end larger conflicts and to pursue those who break the international peace remains unlikely.

Regional organizations could secure peace – NATO, for example, in Europe – but it would scarcely be advisable to rely on this happening. The Western European Union, for instance, missed the opportunity to coordinate the deployment of European troops in the Gulf War. Had the WEU grasped this opportunity, Europe's contribution to the liberation of Kuwait could have been greater, a matter which would not have been without significance for Europe's position in world affairs. European countries should have done much more. As it was, the timidity then displayed by many of them has considerably weakened Europe's negotiating position *vis-à-vis* the USA and other states – a fact which appears to have escaped the notice of the European governments concerned. Washington, though, now knows on whom it can rely and on whom it can most definitely not rely.

Without a fundamental change in thinking at the UN, the organization will soon have abandoned its original purpose and so have forfeited its *raison d'être*. The least which one is entitled to expect from the UN is a mediating function. For many years there has been a border dispute between Peru and Ecuador which seems tailor-made for settlement through UNO. Astonishingly, ever since the 1820s, when these two states came into existence on gaining independence from Spanish rule, the course of the frontier between them in a jungle region has never been determined exactly. War broke out over this matter in 1941, ending with Ecuador's ceding a large border area to her larger neighbour. Renewed fighting has broken out at intervals since 1981. To settle this question and to prevent possible future hostilities would provide some evidence of UN effectiveness.

The intrinsic purpose of the UN cannot be any less than keeping breaches of the international peace to a minimum. If UNO cannot pull itself together sufficiently to develop into a powerful authority maintaining uncompromising international order, it will lose its only chance of justifying its natural *raison d'être*. It can achieve this necessary stature only if every government breaking international law by aggression is declared an outlaw and treated accordingly.

According to the terms of the cease-fire concluded after the Gulf War, Iraq is obliged to allow UN representatives entry to each and every Iraqi installation where there is a suspicion of research into, or construction of, nuclear and other weapons of mass destruction. Correctly assessing the lack of will on the part of the UN, Baghdad has refused entry, with the result that UN inspectors have simply left the country. Baghdad leaves no one in any doubt about the contempt in which it holds the UN, and in so doing encourages like-minded régimes to behave similarly.

There should be only one possible response to such behaviour by Iraq: Baghdad should be notified that every suspect installation will be either entered by UN inspectors on demand, or destroyed without hesitation. Previously programmed Tomahawk cruise missiles can be sent on their way to Iraq from, among other options, warships in the Indian Ocean. An installation to which entry had been refused could, and should, find itself with only a limited time to continue in existence.

This is the only way to deal with criminal régimes if there is to be any prospect at all of asserting the authority of the United Nations and of earning respect for future situations. 'Tomahawk diplomacy', in fact.

The alternative will be the need to fight more wars later, with immeasurably more suffering than through prompt intervention. If the activities of dangerous régimes are not nipped in the bud, such later wars are likely to see weapons of mass destruction used against the industrial nations.

176

THE ARMED FORCES OF THE FUTURE

A clear division has arisen in the development of armed forces. Unless atomic arsenals actually should be dismantled – and this seems unlikely – twenty-first century governments will have two quite different types of sword in their hands. They will have a nuclear deterrent at their disposal and will be able to deploy smaller, highly trained, versatile and fast-moving élite forces anywhere on earth.

Now that the industrial nations are less engaged in full-scale wars, and more frequently called on to deploy forces for intervention or for peacekeeping, it has become essential for those forces also to be fully trained in guerrilla warfare.

One tendency is to be deplored: the training of women as front line combatants. Among primitive peoples there has been a long history of this, which we have no need to emulate. The Germans and the Japanese both fought the Second World War in notably fearsome manner, yet kept their women strictly away from the firing line. The Soviet Union, on the other hand, threw women into battle alongside the men. Though both sexes are admittedly targets in an age of mass bombardment of the homeland, it is difficult to see women in combat as representing other than an unnatural and retrograde step for humanity.

Where there is no direct point of contact between belligerents (as, for example, in a war between Europe and China), it is possible that a war could be fought out over great distances, entirely by nuclear weapons. This raises the question whether strategic weapons should be united in an independent service under its own high command.

A firm command structure is in any case indispensable. Certainly all strategic weapons, whether launched from the sea, from land or in the air, must be controlled by a single, unified supreme command, which in turn has to be closely integrated with the political leadership. An unequivocal linear chain of command is essential whenever nuclear weapons are used, so that the results of any peace feelers can be instantly translated into action. Russia's

Strategic Rocket Armies have existed as a separate service, placed directly under the country's supreme military command, since 1959. Direct responsibility of the highest command for these forces makes sense, at the same time raising the question whether those submarines armed with nuclear missiles should not be taken out navy control and given the same status as the rocket armies.

Generally speaking, navies and air forces are the services with strategic nuclear missiles at their disposal, while armies are equipped with battlefield and medium range atomic weapons. From antiquity until the present age, army and navy have existed side by side as independent organisms to fulfil fundamentally differing tasks. More and more, their roles are overlapping. The launching of nuclear weapons from submarines against targets on land needs to be coordinated precisely, both geographically and in time, with the operations of land and air forces. With the necessity for error-free overall command, it makes sense for all services to be integrated into a single entity.

The Americans disbanded their Air Force's Strategic Air Command in 1992, placing US atomic bombs under a new Strategic Command which coordinates the deployment of all American nuclear weapons. Without doubt this is the correct way forward.

The airmen's dream of being able to decide wars without bloody land battles remained unfulfilled during the Second World War. Because aerial bombardment was a too imprecise weapon, it was capable of bringing about only a partial breakdown of munitions production while inflicting disproportionate civilian suffering. Instead of readiness to capitulate, as intended, the non-nuclear strategic air offensive caused stiffening of the will to resist and acted as a spur to renewed efforts. The enemy's ability to continue fighting was at best weakened, not destroyed.

To a great extent, the old air force dream was finally realized in the Gulf War of 1991. Allied air forces brought about victory on the ground in more than convincing fashion by putting the enemy air force out of action; destroying munitions and fuel dumps, bridges and other infrastructure elements; cutting communications and command systems; decimating the enemy's armoured forces, and so on. Allied air forces fulfilled their strategic purpose so successfully that they did not even have the opportunity to demonstrate their abilities in tactical roles. With their total mastery of the skies, Allied aircraft were in a position to have decimated the armour of Iraq's strategic reserve, the Republican Guard, before it could advance to engage the forward-racing Allied armour. Before this tactical task could be carried out, Iraq's leaders had already been beaten into asking for a cease-fire. The question remained unanswered whether the tactical use of the latest warplanes really could make a tank battle in the style of the Second World War impossible.

It would be self-delusory to allow oneself to be dazzled by the spectacular successes of the Allied air forces in the Gulf, and to conclude that the airmen's original dream has now become irreversible reality. Success such as in the Gulf can be achieved only when forces are unequally matched. Operations must necessarily take a different course when machines and crews engaged on both sides are of like quality.

To the Allied air forces goes the undeniable credit of making the Gulf War one of the few conflicts in which losses were significantly lower than had been expected before hostilities were joined. From a technical standpoint, the role and success of 'smart weapons', and above all of cruise missiles, makes the Gulf conflict the first in a new generation of wars.

A fighting force capable of conducting this kind of limited 'hands off' warfare enjoys the advantage which a rugby team would have if it were suddenly freed from the law prohibiting the forward pass, while this restriction were still applied to its opponents. Success in land warfare usually demands domination of the crucial ground, as is the case in rugby. In association football, on the other hand, victory can, and frequently does, go to a team which has spent most of the game defending in its own half of the field but has managed a sudden goal or goals at the other end. Forces enjoying mastery of the air and armed with the latest guided missiles can similarly strike decisive blows without territorial domination.

The weak spot in so-called 'smart weapons' is their intrinsic dependence on highly sophisticated electronics, making them vulnerable to electromagnetic interference. Piloted aircraft, too, can be brought down by interference with the on-board computers which control diverse functions of the machine. If an aircraft passes too close to a power station, for instance, the strong electromagnetic field generated by the station can cause the pilot to lose control, perhaps for something like ten seconds. A manned machine might be saved by the efforts and skill of the pilot, but this phenomenon suggests the germ of a defence measure, particularly against pilotless missiles. As long ago as 1967, a rocket on board the US aircraft carrier *Forrestal* was detonated by the electromagnetic field of the vessel's electronics. Well over 100 crew members were killed. In the first five days of the Gulf War, American Patriot anti-ballistic missile systems were fired five times in error by diverse electronic devices nearby, in the hands of their own men. News reports from the Gulf concentrated on the successes of Patriots in shooting down Iraqi SCUD missiles, remaining silent about these misadventures.

The American B2 'stealth' bomber was designed to be undetectable. The aircraft's outside surfaces are such as to make the aircraft invisible to radar, while special engine exhaust systems prevent detection by heat-seeking weapons. B2 technology proved its worth during the Gulf War. Baghdad was raided at night, with Iraqi radar unable to detect the B2s and Iraqi anti-aircraft fire discharged blindly and wildly into empty sky.

This is not the last word. British Aerospace's Rapier ground-to-air missile system can follow the flight of a B2 precisely. The Rapier system was developed specifically as a defence against 'stealth' technology. Britain has developed 'stealth' ships, as well as camouflage for soldiers, vehicles and weapons, to a degree approaching invisibility – proof against heat-seeking systems, as well. Britain's is the only army in the world with the ability to make vehicles 'disappear'.

Reliance on ever more sophisticated electronics can lead to unfounded confidence, to forgetfulness of the fact that vulnerability rises with increasing complexity.

Despite their weak spots, cruise missiles, surprisingly, can pose a much greater threat to the enemy than intercontinental rockets. Thanks to their low flight path, only a few yards above ground, cruise missiles are very difficult to detect on radar. Intercontinental missiles can be not just detected but intercepted by ABM systems. There are grounds for anticipating that most cruise missiles will reach their preprogrammed targets, while the same cannot necessarily be expected of their intercontinental big brothers.

At the turn of the century, only two countries are in possession of the latest cruise missiles: the USA and Britain. There is very little to hinder the expansion of this exclusive circle, since these weapons are inexpensive to produce. Even the on-board computers, which govern preprogrammed flight paths and ensure astonishing accuracy, are easily affordable. Should radar and interference systems be developed to a degree enabling interception of even very low-flying cruise missiles, there remains the simplest of responses to any such defence: saturation.

Cost, on the other hand, makes saturation of the enemy's defence network with intercontinental missiles possible only to a limited extent. *Sustained* saturation will be beyond any country's capability. Any such efforts are likely to drain the resources of the attacker. To escape the earth's gravity, intercontinental rockets must first be accelerated to a speed of 25,000mph, which requires huge and massively expensive motors along with enormous quantities of their costly fuel. For the same financial outlay as only one such rocket, an entire fleet of cruise missiles can be launched, offering the means of hitting a vastly greater number of targets with warheads of devastating power.

The latest generation of cruise missiles can bring about results exceeding those achieved in the Gulf, delivering a half-ton warhead from a distance of some two hundred miles with an accuracy of around ten feet.

Tactical roles will be fulfilled by 'mini' cruise missiles. One such American development is only some two and a half feet long, yet has a range of about sixty miles and is capable of differentiating one target from another – for example, it can tell a battle tank from a radar van. These weapons cost only one two-hundredth of the price of a tank, and can be launched in hundreds from a single aircraft. They promise destruction of enemy armoured formations with minimum effort.

Nuclear weapons, which were evolved originally for strategic purposes, are likely to find tactical employment as battlefield weapons to destroy troop concentrations or to alter terrain in order to hinder enemy troop movements.

Without reliable means of delivering them to their targets, even the most powerful nuclear weapons are of little use to any government. Missile flight must be kept as short as possible, in order to defeat all defensive systems. It is therefore unlikely that we shall see those developing countries harbouring nuclear ambitions launching strikes against industrial powers from the distance of their home territory. Missiles themselves are expensive enough; the technology necessary to bypass the defences of industrial nations is unlikely soon to be within the means of these peoples.

An increasing number of states will deploy submarines to enable nuclear missiles to be launched as closely as feasible to their targets, and where possible without detection. The consequence will be ever more submarines deployed to locate and destroy these attackers. The best, and perhaps only reliable, counter-weapon happens to be another submarine.

Submarine fleets are likely to replace the bomber forces of the Second World War, and are certain to decide some wars on a strategic level. Submarine battles beneath the polar ice to determine the fates of world powers are a distinct possibility. Second-grade countries will want to have submarines armed with nuclear missiles, able to remain concealed anywhere in the world's seas and oceans. This requirement could lead to a war of aggression waged by an inland state against its neighbour to gain access to the sea. Interestingly, none of the present nuclear aspirants has need of such a course. Iraq, Iran, Libya, India, Pakistan, North Korea, Argentina and Brazil all possess a coastline and harbours, though few of these countries can at present afford expensive nuclear submarine systems.

Russia needs foreign currency, and has rusting submarines surplus to requirements. Nuclear missiles and their guidance systems would be available from Russia along with the vessels, though these are very expensive. It is nonetheless feasible for a coalition of states to unite in financing such purchases for joint use. Iraq-Libya or Iran-Pakistan seem likely partnerships, with larger alliances of Islamic countries equally possible. Any acquisitions of strategic submarines by such states would of course alarm the industrial nations severely, and lead to expansion of their own submarine fleets for anti-submarine warfare.

In time, submarines too will be replaced, just as they themselves have supplanted the strategic bomber. The submarine's role will be assumed by weapons launched from space. Russia is unlikely to sell strategic missile submarines to other countries without herself first having such weapons systems in place.

The range of strategic missiles is now so great that there is no target on land which cannot be reached by fire from somewhere underneath the world's oceans. Similarly, there is no part of either the land or sea surface of the globe which cannot be kept under surveillance by satellite. Troop and matériel movements preceding aggression can now come as a surprise only if satellite systems are first disabled – an act which in itself would alert possible victims.

Laser 'cannon' are at present the most promising defence against orbiting satellites, some of which can launch missiles from space aimed at targets on earth. Laser weapons themselves can also be used from satellites in a variety of ways against earth targets. Laser beams can destroy targets, detonate weapons prematurely, interfere with electronics and cripple systems relying on computer technology.

The guided nuclear missile became the *ultima ratio* of the twentieth century. Early in the twenty-first century it may well find itself as relevant to the deciding of strategic issues as the cavalry horse, effectively relegated to the status of so much scrap metal by the laser beam. It is only a development such as this which would make sense of abandoning atomic arms.

Weapons development always ends by strengthening the defence. The invention of nuclear weapons has already enabled even smaller nations to deter larger states from aggression; now the laser 'cannon' promises a significant increase in defensive capability. A laser weapons system carried on board an aircraft can destroy enemy missiles in the first phase of their flight from a distance of three hundred miles or more, leaving the wreckage to fall back on the enemy himself.

Laser technology is continually being extended. The use of laser beams to guide tactical guided missiles proved itself in the Gulf War. Other laser systems can be used against the optical and aiming equipment of enemy tanks, 'blinding' these and putting their weapons out of action without destroying them. Crew members using periscopes or other optical devices can be blinded. This anti-tank weapon has already 'fathered' hand-held infantry arms.

Alarmed at these developments, the International Red Cross, which oversees observance of the Geneva and Hague Conventions, is striving to achieve a ban on all laser weapons systems. Here it should be remarked that temporary blindness, however inconvenient and no doubt painful for the individual, has less severe and permanent effects than, for instance, a burst of machine gun fire, which has never been the subject of any attempted ban.

Such well-meaning proscriptions on weapons can lead to more human suffering than they prevent, by robbing a nation adhering to the rules of its own means of self-defence. An example of this is the effort to ban anti-personnel mines. Such proscriptive endeavours are thoroughly understandable in view of the many civilian victims of these weapons killed or crippled even after the end of hostilities, above all in the Third World. All the same, the fact is that poor countries have few other means of defending themselves than by laying carpets of mines around their settlements. Without these, the mass of the people would in most cases be completely helpless, at the mercy of any attacker. NATO officers who experienced the civil wars in the former Yugoslavia confirm that the Bosnian capital Sarajevo, for instance, was saved from capture by Serb forces thanks to the minefields put down outside the town. A great deal of potential human suffering was averted with the help of these unpopular weapons.

It is not the mines themselves which are to blame for the many post-conflict casualties. Culpable are those who lay the minefields and, as is nearly always the case, fail to make and keep accurate plans of these. An attempt to prevent the dangers arising from such situations was made in 1996 with the signing of an international treaty ruling that anti-personnel mines must be as easy to locate with conventional metal detectors as eight grams of iron. Millions of mines with plastic casings, laid in terrain all over the world, cannot be located with traditional devices.

It is not generally appreciated that three-quarters of all US losses in Vietnam were caused by mines. This fact makes it a little more understandable that in the Gulf War the Americans were reluctant to push through Iraq towards Baghdad. Even in an age of the most sophisticated technology, it is still the p.b.i. which pays the price, whether in defeat or in victory. 'High tech' might keep the enemy away from one's homeland, but once it becomes necessary to operate on hostile soil, any thought of 'hands off' can be consigned to the category of mere wishful thinking for the ordinary soldier.

Pilotless reconnaissance aircraft produced in the US can survey a stretch of front between two and three hundred miles long, collecting pictures of such clarity that they reveal whether an individual on the ground is wearing a hat or is bareheaded. Some of these machines are invisible to radar.

Whatever happens on the ground or on the sea will in future be controlled from the air to such an extent that tank battles are likely to become a thing of the past, along with battles between surface ships and perhaps even aerial encounters. Naval surface vessels now need all to be aircraft carriers of a sort, that is, they require aircraft carrying both radar and weapons systems, to act as both their early warning eyes and their defensive arms. With the increasing integration of operational command at sea and on land, shipborne aircraft will more and more be used against land-based targets.

Data banks are currently being compiled which when completed will contain details of every building on earth. The assembled information will allow computation of the most appropriate weapon and warhead to destroy each structure.

Future bombing raids may well be flown by pilots who are themselves sitting in bombproof shelters underground. Possible developments being researched for the Royal Air Force in the twenty-first century include:

conventional manned bombers with a highly sophisticated 'stealth' quality, which will be proof not only against radar and heat-seeking missiles, but also against Britain's own Rapier technology or similar;

giant transport aircraft, which will launch cruise missiles to their targets from a great distance away – a flying counterpart to rocket-launching submarines;

unmanned bombers, which unlike preprogrammed missiles will still need to be flown, but will be controlled by a pilot sitting at a computer terminal on the ground.

Unmanned aircraft enjoy advantages allowing enhanced performance: the machine's manoeuvrability is no longer restricted by the limitations of human physiology. Aircrews can withstand a maximum of around ten times the force of gravity, after which there is a rapid loss of consciousness. For this reason, speed, angle and degree of steepness of turns in manned aircraft are kept well below the technically achievable limits. With these human limitations no longer a factor, a spectacular increase can be expected in the flying characteristics of the next, unpiloted generation of attack aircraft.

At the same time, with the strategic role of aircraft taken over by the long-range missile, there is no longer any *raison d'être* for the independent air force, which had been conceived for strategic purposes. The tactical and transport tasks which will be assigned to, and expected of, aircraft to support land or sea operations can be most effectively carried out by an air force functioning as part of integrated armed forces. Such unified forces would be subject to a single Supreme Command directing all operations on land as well as at sea. Aerial missions can be fitted seamlessly, as required, into overall operational planning. The wheel has turned full circle, the role of aircraft returning to its starting point of tactical support.

Canada has enjoyed unified armed forces since the 1960s. Britain has undertaken a first step in this direction with the establishment of a rapid reaction force under a unified command set up jointly by the Royal Navy, the Army and the RAF. The spearhead of this force is made up of fighting men from élite units who are capable of operating on any terrain on earth. Called 'pathfinders', these units will be the first to enter a trouble spot and to make contact with the enemy.

Between seventy and eighty per cent of losses in modern wars of movement and in actions to restore peace are sustained by troops engaged in seeking out enemy forces. These are the first to come under fire from concealed positions, the first to step on anti-personnel mines. The high percentage of losses of legs, arms, eyes and life suffered by those units first making contact with the enemy may be reduced through the use of recently developed robots equipped with video cameras, which can be sent forward to transmit pictures of terrain and enemy positions. The microwave and infrared sensors of these devices can detect any movement, locating not just enemy soldiers, but mines and other equipment, and even poisons. Inexpensive to manufacture, such 'telerobots' are destined to become commonplace on the battlefield.

The trend towards highly trained élite forces in no way foreshadows an end to massed armies, which will remain necessary at least for defence of the homeland. Even without nuclear weapons, modern armies possess devastating firepower. A multiple rocket launcher which was deployed in the Gulf against the Iraqis can fire twelve missiles with a range of twenty miles, each scattering no fewer than 644 small bombs of diverse types, armour-piercing varieties among them. A battery of such weapons can wipe out all ground targets, including tanks, within an area of about 250 acres. They offer little in the way of accuracy, but the scatter effect makes this unimportant. These systems are particularly effective when used in conjunction with conventional cannon. The latest artillery pieces offer massively greater firepower than their predecessors. In the Gulf, sixty five-inch and twelve eight-inch Royal Artillery howitzers, supported by twelve multiple rocket launchers each firing twelve missiles – in all, eighty-four weapons needing to be manned – supplied four to five times the firepower provided by 882 guns manned at El Alamein in 1942 – an average fifty to sixty times increase in potency per weapon.

In one case at least, cooperation between a nuclear-armed nation and a prosperous country of the non-aligned 'Third World' has led to an interesting technical development. A new rocket with multiple warheads containing conventional high explosive (a British-Chilean design) has even more destructive power than a small atomic bomb. It can devastate an area of forty acres from a distance of twenty to thirty miles.

Alongside a drastic reduction in their nuclear arsenals, the USA and Russia have also agreed to dispose of the greater part of their stocks of old chemical weapons. In all, some 70,000 tons of these lethal agents are subject to this agreement – a quantity theoretically sufficient to destroy all human life six hundred times over.

At least in theory, biological weapons are anything between ten and one hundred times more lethal than these old chemical agents. Their disadvantage is that most are uncontrollable and can endanger the user as well as his enemy. This risk of an 'own goal' is the principal factor inhibiting 'conventional' biological warfare (spreading botulism, smallpox, plague, anthrax and so on). Unlike chemical agents, biological weapons are not dispersed in the atmosphere after use, but, on the contrary, multiply.

No such 'boomerang' effect attaches to pathogenic micro-organisms, which it is possible to breed for attack only on members of a certain race or races.

Specific medical vulnerabilities exclusive to particular races have their origins in the differing genetic compositions of human types – the outcome of thousands of generations of mutations and adaptation. These weaknesses promise a starting point for the cultivation of new bacterium or virus types which will kill the enemy while leaving one's own people unaffected.

Geneticists estimate that some six thousand different illnesses may be unleashed by damage to a single gene. Developing means of launching attacks on a gene possessed by only one group of people can be a matter of no more than a few years. The genes to be targets of assaults are among those found on the short arm of the X chromosone (at a locus designated Xp11.23). Researchers have already identified not only genes which separate Jews from Arabs, but even ones distinguishing some Arab peoples, for example Iraqis, from their cousins in other Arab countries. This, we may be sure, is not the end of the story.

It is possible, for example, to imagine the development of pathogenic bacteria which would wipe out all the peoples of this earth except for the 'yellow' races (who of course are not really yellow).

Anyone tempted to dismiss such ideas as too fanciful should bear in mind that the same contemptuous rejection would have awaited any prophecy made in the 1930s that attempts would soon be made to destroy a people by means of mass gassing on an industrial scale.

THE NUCLEUS OF THE MATTER

Not until fifty years later did the lessons emerging unmistakably from the American Civil War penetrate the consciousness of the world's military. The immediate advantages conferred by the invention of railways, telegraph and the machine gun were recognised readily enough, yet the battlefield revolution which these technical advances had enforced was inexplicably overlooked.

Between them, machine guns and vastly improved artillery meant that the Civil War introduced a new era of destructive firepower which put a bloody end to the accustomed advances over open ground. Trenches now became the norm, while cavalry charges disappeared. Horses could be used only for transport; on making contact with the enemy it had become necessary to dismount and to fight on foot. The machine gun meant the end of cavalry.

Europe's armies took no notice of all this, despite the fact that plentiful reports of events in America were freely available to all – including the newspaper-reading civilian. European soldiers continued to train for battle drawn up in rank and file and even in colourful uniforms. The British learned in the Boer War to exchange their red tunics for khaki, but in general it was not until 1914 in north-eastern France and Flanders that the belligerents ran headlong into the Carnoustie effect, forcing them to absorb the lessons which had been there fully fifty years earlier for all to see.

After this, it should come as no surprise that more than fifty years after the invention and first deployments of the atomic bomb and the supersonic rocket the effects of this technology on the nature both of armed forces and of warfare itself have still not been fully grasped. In considering these implications, it is reasonable to assume that nuclear arsenals will continue to exist, despite the intentions avowed at the United Nations.

For battlefield tactics always to lag behind the possibilities offered by advances in weapons technology is a factor rooted in the inadequacies of human nature. Until now, the price for this inertia of mind has been paid by only one side in war – by the side, of course, which has been the slower to grasp and implement new opportunities. Failure to understand the role of modern weapons of mass destruction, on the other hand, threatens to demand payment of the full price by *both* sides.

There is no room for a way of thinking which sees any future war between nuclear-armed states as a kind of intensified Second World War. To regard atomic weapons only as a reinforcement of one's arsenal, to assume that one can simply dispose of an enemy by means of a nuclear first strike – such an attitude of mind is suicidally dangerous.

Surprise is half of the attack. A sudden assault with nuclear weapons will, however, not necessarily bring with it the usual advantages of surprise. A state capable of hitting back with its own nuclear arsenal, even as it is itself going under, will be able to take its assailant down with it. A first strike on an opponent armed with nuclear weapons can mean national suicide, even if that strike is itself successful. To ensure that a nuclear arsenal survives an enemy's first strike, enabling response with a so-called second strike, strategic weapons are either dispersed, kept permanently on the move (chiefly on board submarines) or stored in hardened bunkers proof against atomic warheads.

Until the end of the Cold War, the Soviets kept 6,600 strategic weapons on the ground, with only 3,800 on board submarines. In almost directly inverse proportions, the Americans maintained 6,200 strategic warheads distributed among their submarine fleet, with no more than 2,450 on land. These dispositions gave America distinctly better chances than the USSR of having her arsenal survive a first strike and of delivering a second strike to nullify the advantage of an enemy's aggression.

It should not be overlooked that attacks on centres of government, communications and command can easily allow an atomic war to run out of control. Nuclear detonations release intense electro-magnetic radiations which can paralyse modern communication networks. Command structures – and these are essential to break off hostilities as well as to direct them – are now more vulnerable to collapse than has been the case in earlier wars.

There would be something to be said for restricting attacks on command centres to those of the lower echelons, sparing seats of government and supreme command so that negotiations remain possible. Against this, there will always be the temptation to carry out a first strike on the enemy's command and communications systems, to deprive him of his capacity to launch a retaliatory second strike. It is nothing more than elementary to ensure that all components of the political and military command structure are proof against nuclear attack.

Around two hundred nuclear weapons detonated on the industrial centres of either Russia or the United States would in each case kill about one third of the country's population and destroy two thirds of its industrial capacity. These would be the immediate effects of the attack, through explosion, heat and radiation, and would represent the level of destruction intended to bring about a cessation of hostilities. Long-term suffering through illness, hunger and damage to the infrastructure would add to the effects but would not immediately strengthen the arguments in favour of a cease-fire.

The differing strengths of these arguments, and their disparate capacities to convince, separate not only the nuclear-armed states from those without atomic weapons. Varying ability to intimidate also distinguishes one country equipped with nuclear weapons from another.

Let us attempt to create a little clarity in this field.

A country possessing atomic weapons does not automatically advance to the status of a nuclear power. We should regard as nuclear *powers* only those states which are capable of inflicting an unacceptable level of damage on the *strongest* state on earth. Only when this ability is acknowledged and respected by the most powerful states can there be any question of credible deterrence, which alone confers the status of an atomic *power*.

Other nations possessing atomic weapons should be regarded simply as nuclear *states*. The Ukraine, Kazakhstan and Belarus, for example, have large stocks of nuclear arms, but those remaining after a programme of dismantling are nearly all short-range missiles and as such without strategic significance.

If we accept this rule of thumb, we see that the twenty-first century is beginning with no more than the same five nuclear *powers* who were the earliest members of the atomic weapons club. Even the two smallest of these powers, Britain and France, have sufficient numbers of strategic weapons in their hands to inflict a deterrent amount of destruction on anyone.

Even so, there are severe distinctions to be made between these five. Inflicting an unacceptable level of damage is one thing; surviving an opponent's strike is quite another. Neither Britain nor France is large enough in either land area or population to absorb the full impact of another power's nuclear arsenal and remain capable of fighting on. This brings us to the very nucleus of the matter.

To render the enemy incapable of further resistance has classically been regarded as the object in war. The concept is inadequate.

This is another area in which Clausewitz needs to be deleted from the thinking of future belligerents, this time with his maxim *'that the disarming or overthrow of the enemy... must always be the aim of any act of war'*.

The sole aim in war can only be to render the enemy incapable of fighting, *while oneself remaining capable.*

Possible objections, that Clausewitz must have meant this, miss the point. Living in a pre-nuclear age, Clausewitz could never have imagined the possibility that conducting a successful campaign could render oneself helpless. An 'own goal' of this kind would have been simply inconceivable to him. We, on the other hand, being able to recognize this possibility only too clearly, are forced to acknowledge the limitations of war as an instrument of state policy.

For Clausewitz, a nation at war was – like that rare creature, the sensible gambler – risking only as much as it could afford to lose. Defeat meant the loss of men, of financial means, perhaps of some territory. Before commitment to war, the prospect of these potential losses would be weighed against the likelihood of possible gains. Never could Clausewitz have countenanced placing the very existence of the nation as a stake.

We fail in our thinking if we do not allow nuclear weapons to impart another dimension to our studies, if our reflections do not operate on a completely different level. Once we take this trouble, one of the first things which we realize is that Britain and France form a sort of sub-species among nuclear powers. Their survival as nations depends on their capacity to *ward off* enemy assaults; for simple reasons of space they cannot withstand repeated nuclear attacks which hit home. China, Russia and the USA, on the other hand, are physically capable of survival. While the USA has only 458 inhabitants per square mile, France has 1,729, with the compact area of the UK groaning under the horrendous figure of 4,056.

Physical capacity to survive is of course a completely different matter from the moral will to go on fighting after destruction of one's homeland. In this respect, the Americans are likely to be found a long way behind the Chinese and the Russians.

We can already perceive the emergence of a graduated scale in the prospects of surviving a nuclear war: China and Russia have the best chances, followed by the United States, with Britain and France bringing up a dismal rear. Interestingly, were these powers actually to renounce nuclear arms, their relative prospects of surviving all-out *non*-atomic war would still emerge in the same sequence.

Far from any expectation of survivability, other states which have acquired nuclear weapons do not even enjoy deterrent capability, except towards their non-nuclear neighbours. Among these, Israel is in easily the best position, being able to deal with any aggressor from her own part of the world. If we ignore terrorist methods, it is clear that none of the other aspirants in the atomic field possesses the capability of launching nuclear attacks on industrial nations. North Korea is probably the only one of these countries which in time might develop effective delivery systems, enabling her to attack, say, Japan. Of the other *de facto* and would-be nuclear states, Libya has fifty per cent illiteracy, while in both India and Pakistan only a minority is able to read and write. North Korea, Argentina and Brazil are admittedly much more advanced, but Iraq, Iran, Libya, India and Pakistan are all without the industrial base essential for a protracted war against even a medium-sized enemy in their own part of the world. India, for one, is unlikely to break out of this intellectual poverty in a hurry; fifty years after her government pledged (in 1950) to introduce universal education within a decade, India still has sixty-seven million children who do not attend school. Her rulers have accorded higher priority to possession of atomic weapons.

Among these ambitious countries, too, a 'league table' of sorts can be discerned. Their atomic weapons give them only a regional status, not irresistible political influence.

Recognizing these basic facts enables us to look at the world with clear eyes and to consider with unfogged minds its shifting constellations of physical strength and moral power.

It can be of no surprise to anyone that despite repeated conflicts in their vital interests, powers armed with nuclear weapons have so far managed to refrain from going to war against one another, whereas on the other hand the succession of wars between non-nuclear countries shows no sign of ending.

Less understandable is the large number of occasions on which countries without nuclear weapons have not shrunk from risking war against the nuclear-armed. Admittedly, in none of these cases has atomic weapons been used. The worldwide condemnation which would be aroused by a nuclear strike against a people not similarly armed has until now sufficed to restrain the nuclear powers. Calculating minds in the Third World know only too well how to exploit these inhibitions, so that if the nuclear powers are to exercise any deterrent or other influence, this will continue to be achieved, if at all, by the potency of their non-nuclear forces

It is a situation which no one could have envisaged at the start of the nuclear age: a power armed with atomic weapons can be disregarded by a state without them.

On the other hand, a nuclear power itself will respect only another similarly armed. Atomic weapons are responsible for there having been no war since 1945 between the ideologically opposed great powers, despite their rivalry for world leadership. This fact does not of course reflect any triumph of diplomatic wisdom and insight, but rather illustrates a reluctance towards suicide.

War was defined by Clausewitz as *'an act of violence, to force our opponent to do our will'*. We find a tendency to refrain from this act when the opponent is another nuclear power. The mere thought of the effects of nuclear war tends to induce a readiness to compromise, to find a solution to international problems without the step into war.

Once hostilities have started, they tend to exact costs well in excess of those which both sides would beforehand have regarded as an acceptable price to settle the issue. Deterrence is always to be preferred – and is cheaper than any armed conflict, in terms of both human suffering and material losses. The so-called 'balance of terror' as in Cold War days was, and will remain, always preferable to 'hot' war.

It is only the introduction of today's weapons of mass destruction which has brought mankind its first spark of hope after countless millennia of self-mutilation and butchery. At one stroke, the invention of the atomic bomb has made the price for military adventures unacceptable. For the first time in history, an aggressor must reckon with disproportionate losses, unjustified by his possible gains, even if he succeeds in imposing his will on the other side. Adventurers considering war are now for the first time forced to refrain from assaults on others equally well armed, if they are not to lose what they already have.

This development represents nothing less than the realization of a universal dream which is as old as organized war itself.

The deterrent effect of nuclear weapons is the latest manifestation of a paradoxical historical tendency. Ever since early man first picked up a bone, a branch or a stone to hit someone, rather than relying on just his own hands, feet and teeth, every weapon has been produced for offensive purposes. Yet the introduction of a more powerful weapon has always ended in strengthening the defence. In the age of the sword, a firearm permitted effortless self-protection. The invention of the machine gun, which fulfilled a centuries-old aspiration, served the defence on both sides in the

First World War to such effect that front lines came to a standstill. Increased firepower had been intended to aid attack; in practice it made it possible for two men to hold up an entire battalion. A nuclear warhead can scarcely be more offensive in nature, yet for more than fifty years it has effectively deterred offensive war, proving to be the ultimate form of defence.

All the same, this peacekeeping quality is nothing more than mere psychological inhibition. It is a barrier which will not hold for ever. To believe that nuclear weapons will exercise their deterrent effect for all time indicates naïvety of the first rank. Whether as a result of calculated aggression, whether 'we all slip into war' once again or, as seems more likely than anything else, through the lunacy or risk-taking of a Third World fanatic newly in possession of atomic weapons, a nuclear war is going to be fought out at some time.

As great as was the fear of war during the 1930s, the British government did not shrink from engagement when it became necessary, despite being convinced that a million civilian casualties would be sustained in the first two days. The paralysing fear of air raids, which for years had acted like a narcotic on foreign policy, was overcome without struggle once it became clear what values were at stake. Reluctance to become entangled in another great war was replaced by the straightforward determination simply to mount more deadly bombing raids than the other fellow.

It is only a matter of time and circumstances for the inhibitions surrounding atomic war to be similarly discarded. All that we do not yet know is when and between whom.

This first atomic war is likely to be limited in duration and scale, above all if it should be started by a Third World country. Should a country ruled by a fanatical régime launch an attack with atomic weapons on a nuclear power, the stronger nation will quickly be able to deal with the aggressor. Such an assault would not be fatal to the victim, though inflicting wounds on an unprecedented scale.

The intimidating effect of nuclear weapons, the general horror felt since 1945, begins to disintegrate as soon as we discover that more Japanese were killed by non-nuclear air raids on Tokyo than by the atomic bomb on Hiroshima. A first acknowledgement that the psychological barrier was capable of being broken occurred during the Korean War. The Americans considered the use of nuclear weapons against the Chinese, but discarded the notion when they realized that such action would squander the deterrent effect while probably failing to achieve the required strategic success (too few atomic bombs; too many Chinese).

H.G. Wells had predicted the invention of nuclear weapons as early as 1914. A general atomic war, he Wells, would cut the world population by half. Fears along these lines expressed since 1945 differ widely. Where Europe is concerned, experts concur with Wells, reckoning with losses of between forty and sixty per cent. The Americans expect to come off rather better, anticipating losses at home of some thirty per cent. The Russians are more confident still, calculating that except in the case of a totally unexpected attack, they could keep their losses down to five per cent.

Surprise attacks, though, are increasingly more likely. Ten hours of warning were potentially available during the 1950s, this being the duration of a bomber flight between the USA and the USSR. With the introduction of the first intercontinental missiles, this margin for warning shrank abruptly to thirty minutes. Since the early 1970s, the flight time of a strategic missile has been cut to something between six and ten minutes, according to the location of the target. This reduction, which practically invites an attempt at surprise attack, has been made possible by deployment of the strategic submarine. As time goes by, ever more second-rank states will want to put nuclear-armed submarines into service, since these can remain hidden anywhere in the world's oceans.

It has to be assumed that a nuclear war will cause a high degree of anarchy within the belligerent states. Civil administration is likely to collapse, with national life scarcely able to continue. Industry, transport and communications will be largely destroyed; supplies of food, power and·water cut off in places; the effects of the worst Second World War air raids (Hamburg, Dresden, Tokyo, Hiroshima, Nagasaki) greatly exceeded, with little opportunity to make good the damage. Researches have shown that even if nuclear strikes were confined to military and industrial targets, there would still be seventy to eighty per cent as many civilian casualties as through deliberate attacks on residential areas. Thanks to the intimate interweaving of militarily important industries with a modern society, nearly fifty per cent of all US citizens, for example, live in places which for strategic reasons have to be among the first targets of an enemy. It is easy to imagine the sort of breakdown in social order to be expected as a result of such conditions – in as far as a civil society continues to exist at all.

In such circumstances, top priority has to be accorded to survival of a central command structure whose lines of communication with its own forces are not broken, and which remains capable of negotiation with the enemy and contact with any allies or neutral states.

Until the end of the 1960s, the USSR would have needed some thirty per cent of her nuclear arsenal simply to cripple the telephone and communications centres of the United States. Today, two to three per cent of Russia's atomic weapons are sufficient to destroy these same systems. Once a government has been eliminated (victim of a first strike), the war will be continued by military commanders, more or less automatically, according to a preprogrammed command scheme.

It is in the interests of both sides for governments to survive.

Leaders of some kind are always necessary to break off a war. To this end, the governments of all the leading nations have a network of nuclear command shelters at their disposal. These have their own generating systems and radio transmitters and are interconnected below ground. It is assumed that television systems will no longer function in a nuclear war, but battery-powered radios will enable survivors to receive announcements and instructions from their governments.

There are of course no shelters available for the mass of the population, but only for members of government, military command personnel and some selected leading civil administrators. Should the balloon go up, the citizens of Switzerland are in the best position. Since the 1960s, a far-seeing Swiss law has required every new house to be provided with a nuclear shelter for its occupants.

What people have once withstood, however terrible it might be, they know that if necessary they can endure again, no matter how devoutly they may pray to be spared a repetition. Irrespective of how firm the resolve 'never again', once the first experience of nuclear war has been survived, this will take its place in the human psyche as a familiar and expected occurrence. Once the current threshold of inhibition has been crossed, people will quickly adjust to the new possibilities now open to them to alter the international power structure radically to their own advantage, and even to bring about a drastic change in the distribution of the world's population. The use of nuclear weapons will become just one of the options available as a matter of course, no more to be eliminated from warfare than was artillery in the wars of recent centuries. Against this, wars among the most advanced states will be fought less often, and only for great gain or in defence of the greatest values.

The destruction of a small country may deter other weak states from engaging in suicidal folly, but it will give larger, more calculating nations ideas.

Though the course of a 'Third World War', should there really be one, is unlikely to be as destructive as an anxious public imagines, it will be devastating enough. Not only the West, but Russia as well could unleash their complete nuclear arsenals against China, and Chinese troops would continue to move forwards. China is in a position to absorb human losses on a scale which would mean final extinction for any Western state, and possibly for Russia too.

The twentieth century's technological innovations have not only enabled peacekeeping through deterrence; at the same time they have opened the way to completely new methods of waging war – and not just by rapid destruction of one's opponent. The spread of nuclear physics and its technology has made possible a new form of warfare: terrorism on a hitherto unknown scale. Even states which are technologically not very far advanced can be in a position to smuggle the components of one or more atomic weapons into an 'enemy' country (perhaps in a diplomatic bag), to assemble and to detonate the device there. Fanatic régimes never lack either the degree of unscrupulousness or the volunteers necessary.

Experience to date does not suggest that dictatorships have greater reluctance to accept casualties among their own people than do democracies. On the contrary, it has to be assumed that leaders who are accustomed to trample all over their citizens are immune to normal humane sensibilities. An authoritarian régime looking for territorial expansion will be able to consider destroying its foreign policy opponent even at the risk of sustaining massive losses itself. Nothing in the history and nature of mankind rules out such an action. Such a calculating course would, however, require the aggressor to be significantly stronger than the rival whom he seeks to destroy.

Anyone looking merely at statistics might easily be alarmed. By the time of the Cuba confrontation in 1962, America's nuclear stockpile was already equivalent to 500,000 Hiroshima bombs. Today, the arsenals of America and Russia between them have 2,500 times the detonating power of all the explosive used in the Second World War. Though such a sober statistic may appear terrifying, an analysis of warheads, probable targets and population distribution shows that while one thousand weapons detonated on Russia could kill forty per cent of her population, quadrupling the strike to four thousand warheads would raise the proportion of victims only to fifty per cent.

It is very easy to allow oneself to be dazzled and completely misled by numbers – and by claims such as the fear that nuclear weapons can spin the earth out of her orbit. Each hour that passes, our globe with its atmosphere is absorbing more man-made energy than is contained in all the nuclear weapons on earth. The detonation of all the world's stockpiles would release precisely as much energy as is produced by the world's engines and electrical current in a period of only fifty-two minutes and thirty seconds, hour for hour, day for day. A great deal more than all-out nuclear war will be needed to knock Mother Earth off her axis.

As the example of Paraguay shows, even recovery from massive human losses will be possible, if only slowly. Between 1865 and 1870, Paraguay lost more than sixty per cent of her population in a series of wars fought against her neighbours Argentina, Brazil and

Uruguay. There were only thirty thousand adult males among the survivors. Today, Paraguay has a population in excess of four and a half millions.

The most effective and speediest way to invoke a new world war would be to abolish all nuclear weapons, as the UN proposes. In the long history of mankind, the invention of the atomic bomb has proved to be the first development capable of discouraging not just the strong, but even the strongest, from launching assaults on smaller nations. Until the advent of something deadlier, it is these weapons alone which offer hope of deterring, and if not deterring, of halting, aggression. Campaigners for nuclear disarmament are to be ignored as the anachronistic irrelevancy which they have become – redundant relics of post-Second World War wishful thinking, as worthless in the effort to preserve peace as are flat-earthers to serious geographical study.

A world without nuclear weapons would always place effective power, that is, the means to dictate world events, in the hands of the strongest party. It would mean a return to the lawlessness and escalating destruction of the years before 1945.

POSSIBILITIES

Soon after the Second World War, Liddell Hart predicted that the invention of atomic weapons would make large-scale wars unlikely in future, a whole series of smaller wars being fought instead. As is well enough known, this prognosis has until now proved totally accurate, attacks on nuclear-armed powers being recognized as suicidal.

Unless laser or other weapons can be produced to exert the same deterrent effect, we can expect any dismantling of nuclear arsenals to unleash a return to that same uninhibited rush into frequent war from which all previous generations have suffered.

It is to the introduction of nuclear weapons, and to nothing else, that we owe the preservation of general peace between the rival industrial nations and blocks since 1945. During the second half of the twentieth century, the intimidating effect of atomic weapons enabled humanity's age-old yearning for lasting peace to be fulfilled, ending – temporarily, at least – the repeated outbreak of wars between the older-established nations. We who have experienced this era of European peace can justifiably count ourselves fortunate.

There is, however, an obverse side.

Out of fear of attack with atomic weapons, governments are also avoiding confrontation in situations where a resolute stand would be appropriate. People are understandably less ready to intervene on behalf of others if the price to be paid appears excessive. Nuclear warheads do a lot for peace, but very little for human rights.

The war feared for decades between Russia and the West always remained unlikely, since Russia's conduct of foreign policy is characterized by calculating and careful forward probing inch by inch, with an avoidance of risk. All the same, the danger of a large-scale war encompassing practically the entire world is by no means banished. The course of the twentieth century should by itself be sufficient to make plain how incalculable are people's actions even when the risks are unmistakable.

North America, Europe and China will be the centres of world power in the twenty-first century, with China unquestionably becoming the pacemaker in international events. Russia and other former Soviet states such as the Ukraine will find it difficult to stand aside, should North America and Europe find themselves engaged in joint warfare against China. It is to be expected that, faced with a choice, Russia and her neighbours will join with the West and throw their weight into the scales against China.

Whereas a commonly expressed fear is that such a world war would mean 'the end of human life', future wars of conquest can, on the contrary, prove less bloody than hitherto. Every kind of horrific scenario has been considered in fiction as well as in factual literature, yet the possibility of bloodless conquest after threats with nuclear weapons is generally overlooked.

An exemplary lesson in technological-psychological intimidation is there for us to examine in the effects of *Blitzkrieg*. The Danish government capitulated at once when German forces marched in on April 9, 1940, simply accepting 'under protest' Berlin's demand not to resist Germany's actions. Three-quarters of a century earlier, the Danes had not hesitated to enter the field against the great power of Prussia (Prussian-Danish War of 1864), but in 1940 Copenhagen had been psychologically paralysed by the impact of Germany's ultra-quick victory over Poland.

Blitzkrieg, as introduced by the German *Wehrmacht*, was a form of warfare containing a powerful element of the psychological. It pointed the way to future methods of conquest in an age when the more advanced nations have largely abandoned thoughts of going to war, as much out of fear as from sagacity. Precisely because they *are* more advanced, industrial countries represent the greatest temptation to a conqueror, while their peoples' reluctance to fight is something which future aggressors will be keen to exploit.

'*Operation Weserübung*', Germany's swift occupation of Norway and Denmark in 1940, might well serve as a model for offensive operations carried out against Europe. Using 1940 methods with only one added refinement, paratroops and small units of special forces could occupy all of Europe's key positions within a few days.

The enhancement in the operational scheme would be first to cripple communications and transport systems, power stations, grid networks and the like by means of so-called computer 'hacking'. This same technique, used to introduce a 'virus' to cause computer breakdown, can also provide access to the enemy's own data concerning his strengths and dispositions. The value of such assaults on data banks (so-called cyber warfare) can scarcely be over-estimated.

This is one of the principal areas in which over-confidence in one's own technical systems can be the prelude to total disaster. The most sophisticated computer network defences, including military ones, have proved vulnerable even to schoolboy hackers. There are no national boundaries in cyberspace, no distances or geophysical obstacles to be overcome.

The introduction of the internet has rendered every advanced country more vulnerable to crippling of its vital functions by computer virus than they were to the bomber aircraft fleets of World War Two.

Stanley Baldwin, three times Britain's Prime Minister between the world wars, had served for ten years as Chief of the Air Staff. Baldwin's experience led him to summarize the difficulties of air defence with his maxim that 'the bomber will always get through'. It is imperative for us to accept from the outset that the hacker will always get through.

Alternative systems must be not only in place, but also in regular peacetime use alongside vulnerable computer-controlled structures. Only in this way can there be assurance of familiarity and effortless continuity of operation should electronic networks be crippled.

Once a victim has been largely paralysed, the main weight of military operations will be directed against his sites of weapons deployment, ammunition depots, troop contingents, centres of government, command and communications centres, signals networks, sites of munitions production and the like. The object will be to destroy weapons sites, troops and government centres, while capturing ammunition depots, research facilities, weapons development centres and factories.

After the Second World War, the Western Allies kept quiet about the decisive role which interception of enemy signals had played in their victory. In the air, in all operations on land and in the critical U-boat battles, the German *Wehrmacht* was fighting under the greatest handicap imaginable next to the annihilation of its resources. The Allies were precisely informed of every German action and intended action. This priceless advantage was due to the British ability to read enciphered *Wehrmacht* radio signals in plain text, alongside a sophisticated system of aerial photoreconnaissance – two tools keeping the Allies abreast of every German move.

It was clear to the Germans from the unpleasant surprises which they continually experienced in battle that the Allies were being kept in the picture, and they ascribed this to widespread treason on their own side. Field Marshal Rommel, for example, suspected that a traitor within the high command of his Italian allies was responsible for his reverses in North Africa. This was not the case. Thanks to photoreconnaissance and their reading of the German's own radio signals, the British knew, among other matters, of the departure and course of every transport ship carrying desperately needed supplies to Rommel's hard-pressed fighting men. The sinking of these ships by the RAF and the Royal Navy determined the strategic outcome.

What ensured Allied victory then will continue to turn the scales in future. Warfare will increasingly become a battle of information and electronics.

The battleground has shifted. Clashes between forces in the field generated the race to produce arms and the bombing of industrial centres. Defence exertions have now become a contest between scientists. Preventive murders of scientists and technicians engaged in various fields of weapons development can not only not be ruled out; they are likely to become a defensive necessity. No government fearing for the safety of the state will find any difficulty in justifying such murders: the deaths of individuals, to preserve the lives of millions. Few people will have difficulty in responding affirmatively to the question: would it have been defensible to have assassinated Adolf Hitler in 1938? Assent to this issue already asserts the moral principle. The only difficulty remains in assessing the degree of risk from future potential Hitlers.

Murders of scientists and development engineers promise perhaps the ultimate form of the strategic pre-emptive strike. Preventive assassination of a dangerous national leader or other political personality can have serious diplomatic effects, whereas the violent death of a scientist might occur without political consequences, not least since the opportunities are likely to be greater for disguising it as an accident. A number of British experts engaged in development work on advanced weapons systems died in unexplained circumstances (car crashes without witnesses, and the like) during the 1980s.

On March 22, 1990, an assassination squad from the Israeli *Mossad* secret service shot dead the Canadian gun designer Dr. Gerald Bull in Brussels. Bull was working on the construction of a so-called super-cannon for the Iraqi dictator Saddam Hussein. He had already built a weapon which had fired a shell to a height of 112 miles – a world record. Bull believed it possible to fire a shell from Montreal to Mexico City (a range of some 2,500 miles), and wanted to send an atomic weapon by cannon into satellite orbit round the earth – a significantly cheaper launching system than the rocket. Bull claimed that he was already capable of firing shells over a range of more than six hundred miles. Any such development would have enabled, say, Tel Aviv (only some five hundred miles distant) to be bombarded from Baghdad with greater accuracy than by rockets.

From his design centre in Brussels, Bull helped China in developing her artillery. Iraq bought Bull designs which could fire shells thirty-five miles high. Some Bull cannon were procured by Baghdad from South Africa, where they had originally been delivered. These were the transactions which led to Bull's death.

Should weapons experts from the former Soviet Union enter the service of Arab countries, further assassinations along the lines of Dr. Bull's may be expected. Computer experts, 'hackers' and others capable of crippling national command and control systems are similarly obvious candidates for such pre-emptive actions.

Future operations will be given an additional dimension by the inclusion of a terrorist element. Offensive undertakings will become a combination of commando raids and terrorist attacks, with the likely abduction or assassination of political leaders. Blackmail of one sort or another is likely to be a dominant feature of future invasions.

Such operations are conceivable even without the use of atomic weapons, though no nuclear-armed state would hesitate to strike back with atomic weapons even against a non-nuclear attack, if this attack were to threaten its continued existence.

Even if only Europe were to be under actual attack, the encirclement of North America by strategic submarines would be a matter of course. Such action would be accompanied by simultaneous threats on the one hand (nuclear attack in the event of US 'interference' in European events) and conciliatory promises on the other (for example, an early withdrawal of forces from Europe).

The view is frequently expressed that since the collapse of the Soviet Union the West no longer has any enemies. It is argued as a consequence that NATO countries have no further need of great armaments. It is forgotten that Western nations might not necessarily be confronted by an enemy directly, but that they must reckon on having to defend their interests and fight on behalf of other peoples in many different crisis territories.

It should not be difficult for anyone to imagine where, for instance, the demand of Muslim extremists for an Islamic world state might lead, particularly should a fundamentalist Islamic régime come into possession of atomic weapons.

How Russia might develop internally and behave towards the outside world remains a matter requiring close observation. It is nonetheless quite conceivable that Europe, rather than being compelled to fight against Russia as was expected for so long, will instead find herself fighting *alongside* Russia to stem an invasion from Asia.

Europe has been under pressure from Asia for as long as recorded history. In the years between 492 and 449 BC, the sacrifice of greatly outnumbered Greek warriors prevented the overrunning of southeastern Europe by Persians spreading a cruel régime. Without this successful defence, the doors to the whole of Europe would have been opened to Asian behaviour patterns, and European development – not least in respect of ethical and humane values – would have taken a quite different course.

Only bitter resistance by Germanic and Roman armies put an end in the fifth century AD to the advance of the Huns, who had created a trail of devastation even as far west as the Marne. The Arabs inflicted great destruction in their eighth and ninth century attempts to annex Spain, France and Italy for the Islamic world. Charlemagne threw back the Avars towards the end of the eighth century; the German Emperor Otto the Great frustrated the westward march of the Magyars in 955. Christian civilization in Europe narrowly escaped destruction in 1241, when the Mongols pushed as far westward as the outskirts of Vienna.

The next threat from Asiatic invaders observing different ethical standards came in 1354, with the leap of the Turks across the Dardanelles. Within a few decades, the Turks had pushed as far into Europe as Sarajevo; in 1529 they stood, like the Mongols before them, just outside Vienna. It was the Austrians who now twice saved Europe from catastrophe: not just in 1529, but again in 1683, when the Turks once more laid siege to Vienna without success. The Europeans' technical superiority in developing musketry and artillery played the decisive role here in putting an end – for the next few centuries – to more than 2,000 years of repeated invasions by Asiatic hordes.

Today, the organization and running of industrial countries can be paralysed without the need for physical invasion. A single Third World computer hacker will one day be in a position to wage his own crippling assault – a Thermopylae in cyberspace.

The same primitive urges which impelled earlier invasions – envy and greed – have not been expunged from the world. They are likely to continue to spark future wars, so long as there are under-armed nations enjoying a higher standard of living than their neighbours.

All earlier civilizations, including the Roman, fell victim to barbarian assault. Only a few decades before turning their attentions to Europe, the massed cavalry hordes of the Huns had invaded highly developed China from the north.

More advanced peoples continually suffer assault from the less fortunate. Singapore, for example, rich in industry, is surrounded by such dangers. Though Singapore maintains only very small armed forces for defence, her flourishing economy includes a young arms industry, some branches working in highly sophisticated technical fields, including rocket technology. It is these industries which constitute a tempting objective for other Southeast Asian states less well blessed and looking for expansion.

Other potential wars can be identified in diverse continents:

between Vietnam and Cambodia over border disputes;

between India and Pakistan for possession of Kashmir;

between Sudan and Uganda, whose governments accuse one another of supporting revolutionary armies on each other's territory;

between Ethiopia and Eritrea over one hundred and fifty square miles of disputed stony ground at the border;

between Somalia and Kenya over disputed border regions;

between Nigeria and Cameroon over oil rights;

between Ecuador and Peru also over a disputed frontier;

between Greece and Turkey over Cyprus. The last such battles between these two cost five thousand lives.

Religious wars can also be expected, including internal ones such as, for example, between the Muslim minority and the 560 million Hindus in India. Any such eruption is likely to draw Pakistan into the fighting.

Far more significant than all of these quarrels will be the course taken by China with her ever-growing population. If China cannot feed her people, her armed and hungry millions will cross their country's borders into the spaces of Mongolia and perhaps Siberia, just as into India and the fertile lands of all Southeast Asia. Not just the richer industrial states of the East, such as Singapore, Taiwan and South Korea, but Japan, too, that economic and technological world power, is likely to become an object of irresistible desire for a China which is overpopulated and underfed yet armed with nuclear weapons.

America's reaction to any Chinese attempt to annex Japan is likely to determine the further course of the twenty-first century. The poorer countries of the region – among them Thailand, Burma and India – will also appear on China's 'shopping list' thanks to their food harvests.

Chinese invasions of Mongolia and Russia's eastern regions cannot be excluded, and this would not be without effects on Europe. Should Russia meanwhile have become a member of NATO, as a Moscow government representative said on May 14, 1990, that she wanted to do, then all other NATO nations would in such an eventuality be obliged to go to war against China.

For régimes based on contempt for individual human beings, weapons of mass destruction – not only atomic warheads, but chemical and above all biological weapons as well – open up ways to expand their power of which they could previously only have dreamed.

An aggressor will always try to occupy the territory which he covets, while damaging it only as little as is necessary. Just as a burglar would scarcely set fire to a house which he intends to plunder, so no aggressor intends to destroy those very cities, industries and infrastructure which he wishes to add to his possessions. An aggressor wants simply to remove those people who stand in his way.

It is rather the victims of aggression who in the blind rage of their hatred and fear tend in hitting back to unleash thoughtless destruction of an enemy country and people. This drives the price of aggression so high in case of failure that it should give any potential aggressor considerable food for thought. On the other hand, fanatical governments, whether of religious or ideological character, provide us with no grounds for supposing that they will either calculate or act soberly.

211

Most wars of conquest have until now been waged to gain not only territory but also other subject peoples, if not as slaves then at least as underlings whose work would strengthen the state. As we enter the third millennium of the Christian era, there is no shortage of potential human labour anywhere on earth. What are scarce in many places are food, consumer goods and a fully developed mature infrastructure. It tends therefore not to be the neighbouring people who constitute a temptation, but only their land and everything *not* human which is on it.

Subjugation of other peoples no longer needs to be the objective of a war of aggression; on the contrary, many states can now regard the populations of other countries simply as disposable objects.

Let us imagine for example an Asiatic power whose population grows to such an extent that acute food shortages threaten to bring about the country's collapse. Modern mass-destruction weapons offer the leaders of such a power the means of clearing other, fertile countries of their current inhabitants, in order to settle their own people there. For such a purpose, neither nuclear nor chemical weapons are necessary, or even suitable, since they would pollute the land. Biological means are conceivable, for instance pathogenic micro-organisms which would attack the black races but leave the yellow peoples untouched.

Such weapons – negricides, as it were – would leave the way free for the greatest mass migration to date. The population of Africa could become extinct, this fertile continent would become almost uninhabited and the surplus Asian peoples could settle there.

It is not to be expected that western nations would remain inactive spectators at such an action. All the same, the impartial observer would have to tip the Asian power for victory in any nuclear war between East and West over Africa, since the eastern people would be better able to absorb human losses on a massive scale, and would also be readier to accept these.

It need not, of course, come to such a war. Biological means are equally conceivable which would drive the white races into extinction as well. Even simpler would be a weapon which would attack fatally all human races except the yellow ones.

Developments in the field of genetic modification of grain, fruit, meat and vegetables suggest the possibility for foodstuffs-exporting states of spreading heritable defects, illnesses, epidemics or mutations among their customer countries.

The invention of mass-destruction weapons has placed the means within reach to reshape the entire face of our planet within the relatively near future.

Yet are such thoughts not too far-fetched, not science fiction fantasy?

In itself such an idea is nothing new. Genghis Khan is estimated to have exterminated some forty million Chinese during the thirteenth century, to clear the northern regions of China for his Mongols from Inner Asia. This was the origin of the country which we today know as Mongolia and which was established on land freed of its Chinese inhabitants. Anyone who thinks that basic human nature has since then improved to such an extent that any such undertaking would now be unthinkable has obviously not familiarized himself even with the events of his own century.

Nothing which is technically possible is too cruel for man to use against his fellows if it will further his own interests. It is those prognoses anticipating an improvement in mankind, and foretelling a less painful future, which repeatedly prove instead to be mistaken. In defence matters we cannot approach scientific developments and possibilities with less than conscientious realism. It is beyond dispute that the present attainments of science have opened up completely new perspectives for unscrupulous national rulers.

KEEPING THE PEACE

At first sight, the introduction of atomic weapons might appear to be the most horrific aspect of warfare development during the twentieth century. Far more significant – and considerably more worrying – is man's proven inability to learn even from the manifest lessons of such an eventful century.

Surely few leave school without having learned how the triumphalism of the Allies in their brutal treatment of Germany in 1919 led directly and inevitably to the founding of the National Socialist movement and to the Second World War. Blindly spurning the opportunity to learn from these unhappy experiences, many Americans with influential positions affecting US foreign policy can be heard proclaiming triumphantly that the West has 'won' the 'Cold War' and as the 'victor' must pocket some gain from this 'victory'. These experts ask rhetorically in public what is the point of winning a war, if victory does not bring a gain of some kind.

It appears to have escaped the notice of these gentlemen – or else, inexplicably, it is insufficient for them – that the 'gain' already consists both of having for half a century preserved Western Europe from Soviet occupation and the world from a terrible atomic war, and of having finally brought about the collapse of the military power of the Soviet Union through the attrition of the arms race. For decades, these same people dared scarcely to hope for such an outcome, and now they are not satisfied with it. Since mistakes are only human, errors are *per se* understandable and often pardonable.

To repeat a mistake, on the other hand, is less understandable and harder to forgive. Stubborn insistence on expanding NATO, by including as members Russia's former Warsaw Pact allies without Russia herself, is placing Moscow's leaders in the same position in which the Germans found themselves in 1919. In giving the Russians the impression that they are surrounded by enemies, this NATO expansion is nothing more than a powder keg waiting for a detonator – and a completely unnecessary one at that.

Of course, the Russians have themselves contributed to their isolation. Unable or unwilling to restrain their sledgehammer mentality, they set about repressing Chechen strivings for independence with a brutality rightly incurring worldwide condemnation. The degree of tact, or the lack of it, with which the outside world remonstrates with Moscow over such matters will largely determine whether Russia can be persuaded gradually to an acceptable standard of conduct. If we cannot win Russia over to becoming one of the humane and civilized family of peoples, we are likely to drive her ever more deeply into the intransigent, resentful stance of the paranoid 'loner'. Those convinced that everyone is against them are particularly dangerous, and we must live alongside the Russians, as we must alongside everyone else.

By ignoring psychological factors, the error of the Versailles Treaty is being repeated. The other fellow is being humiliated and made to feel that he is regarded and being treated as an outsider and as practically an outlaw. This can only drive him into a defensive posture. In addition, Russia's financial difficulties are remarkably like those of post-First World War Germany. All in all, the Russians find themselves in a situation which they might one day feel that they can escape only by seizing the initiative through war.

Germany's post-Versailles statesmen were forced to eat humble pie, and in view of the punitive nature of the peace terms imposed it was only a question of time before Germany acquired a government committed to rejecting these conditions and exacting revenge. Human nature being what it is, how could it be otherwise?

How can we expect of future Russian leaders anything other than that they too will be driven by unimaginative attitudes and actions into a reactionary nationalism which will one day take revenge on the Western nations? A world stripped of its nuclear arsenals would be a world restrained by fewer inhibitions, while the twenty-first century is starting with the less than promising situation of a Russia forced into the same outcast role as Germany after Versailles.

The sort of small-minded view demonstrated by influential Americans can at best be regarded as a sign of tactlessness. More realistically, it must be condemned as almost criminal arrogance of the kind which has burdened mankind with one unnecessary war after another in practically unbroken succession. On the one hand, too many people, like these American professionals, exercise insufficient imagination. On the other, it is the exact opposite, an excess of fantasy, which has been the cause of immeasurable human suffering. Without his capacity for creative thinking, man would have spared himself an incalculable amount of anguish.

We have only to think of the pain which people have inflicted on one another from the dawn of their history for the sake of some idea or other of whose truth they have convinced themselves. Once, innocent individuals were sacrificed ritually in the belief that their deaths were necessary in order to satisfy some imaginary spirit, perhaps of a mountain or of the sun. Mass slaughter has been the price exacted in countless wars to promote or to defend a religion. Add to these the casualties of ideological warfare in modern times and the numbers of those tortured to death or simply 'liquidated' in the dictatorship of one dogma or another.

All these poor people suffered premature and frequently painful death in the name of something which others had thought up without ever being able to prove that it was correct.

There is no other living creature which mistreats its fellows as much as do human beings. Animals attack others only in order to secure a material advantage, principally food. Since an animal does not inhabit a world of abstract or philosophical thought, it cannot create for itself fantasies of gods or ideas, for the sake of which it feels compelled to be violent towards others of its kind.

As cruel as the animal kingdom might appear to us with its daily fights for survival, the fact is that wildlife sets a good example to man where the avoidance of unnecessary suffering is concerned. Man has evolved a very high capacity for thought which has enabled him to make his life secure and comfortable. Logically, he should be applying that same reasoning power to ensuring that he lives harmoniously among his fellows. Instead, he uses his imagination to invent what he cannot prove, and devotes his energy to fighting about it.

Even normally rational people are capable of irrational behaviour. Faced with a fanatic who is not even usually rational, it becomes several times more difficult to anticipate his conduct and to ensure appropriate counter-measures.

People can, and will, always find a reason to go to war. In July 1969, El Salvador won a qualifying match for the football World Cup against her neighbour Honduras. This result led to riots in Honduras, which ended with the deaths of two Salvadoreans and the deportation of eleven thousand more. Salvadorean troops promptly invaded Honduras, cities were bombed and armoured columns pushed towards the Honduran capital. It was not until sixteen days later that the Organization of American States succeeded in persuading El Salvador to withdraw her troops. This 'football war' cost Honduras around four thousand dead. El Salvador did not just suffer human casualties, but lost an oil refinery to air raids as well.

As incomprehensible as these events may appear to us, we are forced to accept that for the people concerned the motivation was fully sufficient. We are similarly compelled to accept the fact that some peoples display a considerably lower threshold of patience and common sense than that to which we are accustomed. One day, even these less inhibited nations will possess weapons of mass destruction.

In endeavouring to make and to keep the peace, it can prove a literally fatal error to ascribe to other peoples our own humane values and temperaments. However swiftly weapons technology might advance, a fundamental improvement in the human psyche requires aeons. To regard other people and behave towards them as though they were of the same stuff as ourselves, motivated by the same ideals and inhibited by the same feelings, to expect from them the same reactions and conduct, can lead easily to mistakes with catastrophic consequences. Just like individuals, so peoples, too, vary widely in their temperaments, their expectations, their values and their reactions either to temptation or to threats.

It is essential to remember that not all our future battles will be fought as cleanly as were, for example, those in North Africa during the Second World War. There are many peoples incapable of separating the individual soldier from whatever sins his government might be considered to have committed, who treat all opponents as criminal beasts, and who have no interest in, or intention of, taking and keeping alive enemy prisoners. Such peoples, and some are nearer to home than we might think, take prisoners at all for only two temporary purposes: first, for interrogation under torture, and second, for slave labour. With the end of their usefulness, prisoners are routinely killed.

We dare never act as though the world were as we should like it to be, but only in accordance with how it demonstrably is.

All the same, it would be mistaken to take too negative a view of humanity, for all our manifest shortcomings. There are a lot of very clever people out there; if there had not always been, we should still be living in caves, sheltering from wild animals, rather than enjoying the consumer goods, medical care and generally high degree of safety and comfort with which we are currently blessed.

There are also a good many kind and caring persons in the world. Most people worldwide are fundamentally decent, without predatory inclinations and with no object other than to lead their own lives in comfort, safety and happiness, at peace with their fellows. They have no wish to interfere with or to prey on others, and desire nothing more than for their fellows similarly to leave them at peace. Between them, the kind and the clever (who are not always the same individuals) should be able to devise some kind of path to be followed internationally to avoid too frequent bloodshed. The prospects of doing so do not seem bright. The good may never start wars, but they are repeatedly called on to finish them.

Mankind endures more than enough suffering through natural disasters, which are uncontrollable, and through accidents, which may be mostly avoidable but are by definition at least not intended. The self-infliction of yet further suffering through warfare, all proceeding from the conscious, deliberate decision of someone or other, is an offence to whatever dignity humanity possesses and a crime whose prevention is our supreme imperative. Every outbreak of war represents collective abject failure by mankind. The difficulty is that the goodwill of all is necessary to keep the peace.

To unleash a war requires the intractability, ill intent or unpredictability of only one. There is never any shortage of people of a naturally malevolent disposition, and these frequently possess the drive needed to propel them into positions of political power. If mankind is to have a future of less pain than our ancestors have endured, if we are truly concerned for the security and welfare of our descendants, we can leave no effort untried to keep such malevolent leaders in check.

It is tempting to imagine that with the upwardly spiralling cost of weapons, warfare will become priced out of existence, that no nation will even dare contemplate going to war since it would be unable to sustain the effort beyond the first exchange of fire without immediate national bankruptcy. A delightful dream indeed, and while it is unlikely to be realized, there is already a precedent of a sort in the fate of the Soviet Union, bankrupted at the very thought of having to compete with America's proposed Strategic Defence Initiative.

Keeping the peace demands not just all-round goodwill; it is equally essential for all peoples (or at least their leaders) to be motivated by the same ethical values – something which not even in Europe is the case. How far removed we are from a global commonality of standards is illustrated by, among other things, the fact that while more than half of the world's people live in states which are officially 'democracies', less than one quarter of mankind enjoys the elementary right of a free press. 'Democracy', like 'peace', is a much-abused word, having frequently almost nothing whatever to do with those values which we know as belonging to a democracy, and which we find worth defending.

We also have to acknowledge that not all peoples feel the same desire for lasting peace. It is the most advanced nations which, after millennia of mutual self-mutilation, have finally attained the highest degree of insight and wisdom. Developing countries, on the other hand, show little sign of inner yearning for peace, particularly those whose governments or peoples are in the grip of an ideology or a religion. It is these nations, not the industrial countries with atomic weapons, who represent the greatest threat to world peace.

Muslim fanatics, for example, *want* to die in battle for their faith, strong in their belief that death for Islam in battle against unbelievers will take them instantly to Paradise to enjoy their reward in all eternity. The author has heard directly from the lips of Muslim soldiers: 'I would rather die than live'. Such fervour is the unseen part of the iceberg waiting to tear the bottom out of even the most titanic efforts at mediation or at keeping the peace.

A government's wish for peace does not always enjoy the unequivocal support of its people. In the course of the twentieth century the statesmen Michael Collins (Republic of Ireland), Walther Rathenau (Germany), Anwar al-Sadat (Egypt) and Yithzak Rabin (Israel) were all assassinated by fanatics from among their own people after they had striven for, or concluded, peace with those against whom they had earlier fought. These murders were committed out of the all too human reluctance to break with the past. It is difficult to obliterate remembrance of injustices, real or imagined, which a nation has suffered. That such memories should be passed on to each succeeding generation may be understandable, but raising children in a spirit of resentment and hatred will scarcely advance mankind. Such bequeathing of hatred is practised on a widespread scale, not excluding some European countries. If man does not abandon propagandistic indoctrination of this kind, he will never find his way out of that eternal web of warfare which he has spun for himself and in whose grip he remains entangled.

There can scarcely be a more important task for man than the search for peace. Those who devote themselves to the study of international conflicts, arms races and the like, deserve our respect. Despite their well-intentioned efforts, research into peace and war, like the even older investigations into the causes of crime, is likely always to remain an inexact science with scarcely any practical application. Irrespect0ive of the elimination of those unsatisfactory social factors long held to be the wellsprings of crime, every human society will always produce criminals. Even as living conditions improved, crime rates rose in all the industrial nations during the second half of the twentieth century. We should not be surprised if wars prove as difficult to abolish as crime, despite every possible attempt at restructuring international relations by means of disarmament treaties, co-operation agreements, frequent diplomatic conferences and the like.

Just as there are differing kinds of war, so there are varying degrees of peace. What diverse peoples mean by this apparently highly subjective term varies enormously. The *Great Soviet Encyclopaedia*, for instance, defined peace as that state which would be attained once all the nations of the earth had become communist. By this definition, anyone opposing the spread of communist power was an 'enemy of peace'.

Hopes of abolishing war reached their peak during the twentieth century. For the Allies, the First World War was 'the war to end wars'. The shock of that gigantic conflict, with its poison gas attacks and aerial bombing raids, produced 'no more war' movements in most countries. Once these hopes had been destroyed, the International Military Tribunals at Nuremberg and Tokyo made the first attempts at condemning as crimes the planning and waging of wars of aggression. Legal action against the responsible leaders was intended to be a first step towards eliminating war from international life. The UN was founded with great hopes of securing an era of peace and order in the world. Despite this, small and medium-scale wars have never ceased since then, while peace has been preserved in Europe only through mutual fear of atomic weapons.

On the ending of the 'Cold War', influential people who should have known better made great pronouncements about a new epoch of general peace, just as had happened in 1918 and again in 1945.

The notion of permanent solutions is in any case illusory. International relations are not something which can be 'frozen' in what appears to be an ideal state. On the contrary, they are like living organisms, continually subject to changing conditions and the force of events.

These variations in circumstance can have their origins in quite unexpected fields, including those which have *per se* nothing whatever to do with either politics or the military. It is certain never to have crossed the minds of the pioneers of internal combustion engines that their work would one day help to shift the international centre of gravity. Yet this is indisputably the case. The sudden demand for oil brought about by motorization created for many Arab states riches on a scale which at the start of the twentieth century they could not have imagined. The respect now accorded to these Arab oil giants by industrial states without oil reserves of their own was underlined by the Gulf War for the liberation of Kuwait.

In an age of mass-destruction weapons, the combination of great wealth with a possibly militant Islam must provide cause for thought. Any amount of common sense and logic will be helpless in the face of unpredictability, the 'madness' of a national leader, or the effects of an ideology or religion which has mutated into blind fanaticism.

Ignoring for the moment dangers deriving from irrationality, it is self-evident that the most promising means of bringing about an enduring peace is to settle justly those questions which have already led, or can lead, to hatred and resentment. There would have been no Second World War, had the Allies in 1919 paid attention to those wise words which the Spartans directed to the Athenians in 425 BC, after six years of gruelling war:

'Where there is great hatred, there can in our view be no lasting peace if peace is concluded in a spirit of revenge, if one side prevails in war and then forces its enemies to agree to observe the conditions of an unequal treaty. What makes a peace treaty last is when the side which has it in its power to act like this refrains from doing so, and instead adopts a more sensible posture, outdoing the other side in magnanimity and offering a peace on more merciful terms than the enemy had expected. In such a case, the enemy, instead of feeling the need to avenge the wrong done him, will feel obliged to return like for like, and as a result will rather feel morally obliged to observe the terms agreed'.

Every participant in peace negotiations should study these lines – and bear in mind the consequences of ignoring them. The Athenians brushed aside Sparta's well-conceived offer of peace, with the result that the devastating war lasted for a further twenty-one years and ended with the complete downfall of Athens.

The general peace which lasted in Europe for almost a hundred years between 1815 and 1914 argues the validity of the Spartan reasoning. There were smaller wars during those years (Crimea, Prussia and Austria, Prussia and Denmark, Prussia and France, etc.), but none of these spread. The exemplary spell of *general* peace was a consequence of the just treatment of France at the Congress of Vienna, once Napoleon had finally been defeated.

The same charges which were directed at Germany in 1919 could have been levelled with more justification at France after Waterloo. France had been Europe's troublemaker for long enough, and the Allies could understandably have decided that they would split her into a series of smaller states in order to ensure that she never again became strong enough to represent a danger to anyone. Wisely, this was not done. The consequence could only have been that Frenchmen would have reunited and have become powerful enough to fight for revenge within a generation. Where a nation has been humiliated, there is a correspondingly acute psychological need for self-reassertion. The mutilation and degradation of Germany and Austria in 1919, leading inexorably to the events of 1938 and 1939, stand in crass contradistinction to the well-judged treatment of France after Napoleon. The lessons for the future are unmistakable.

Sadly, experience shows that justice is frequently not enough. Countries which lack for nothing, and which no one has mistreated, can set about their neighbours out of sheer greed. This is no different from the thefts committed by the sons of good families ('We can't understand it, officer. We've always given him everything he ever wanted'). The commonality between crime and war cannot be overlooked. One thing does separate them: the crimes of individuals within society have always been rejected as inadmissible behaviour and punished accordingly, while war, the act of an entire community, has until the twentieth century been accepted as a completely normal proceeding.

The acquiescence in war as *'nothing but the continuation of state policy using other means'* by no means began only with Clausewitz. War always was a political means – even, in the beginning, the only means. In the course of time, experience of war made it possible to bend the other fellow to one's will with the threat of war alone. This was the origin of diplomacy to solve difficulties and avoid bloody clashes. The most advanced nations have meanwhile reached the stage where they go to war only as a last resort, for self-defence, to liberate illegally occupied territories or to protect peoples who have been attacked.

Going to war has always been such a matter of course that any power, whether a mediaeval principality or a modern nation state, seems to have felt that exercising its military strength was necessary in order to affirm its own existence. Only its capacity to deploy forces in the field seems to establish the existence of a state as an independent organism (Iceland is an exception in having no armed forces of her own, but she of course lives within the shelter of NATO). The army comes to represent the entire nation, whose self-respect rises and falls with its soldiers' successes or failures. Modern weapons of mass-destruction have not eliminated the need to flex one's muscles, but only inhibit its exercise.

Wars and crime are both unavoidable, because human relationships in any form (and the same applies to many animal groups) are always subject to background tensions which are more or less consciously perceived. These tensions have their roots in the differing wishes and needs of individuals, in the compulsion to assert one's own interests. Suckling piglets in a litter, with no capacity to spare thought for others, will thrust competing siblings aside to satisfy their own need for milk.

Homo sapiens has a choice. He may behave like a pig, and indeed many of the species do. Chiefly, though, he accommodates conflicting desires through understanding, consideration and suppression of selfishness. Even so, at times the natural drive to self-assertion leads to conflict. Clashes of some kind can never be ruled out entirely from the life together of two or more people. Even the best marriages founded on lifelong love will have their moments of disharmony. Conflicts of interests or will can lead to outbreaks of violence even among the smallest groups of people.

Relationships between states are subject to the same natural tensions as are personal ones, and these can never be eradicated. It would be no better than wishful thinking to assume that the degeneration of these tensions into war can always be prevented by well-meaning negotiation and mediation. Pious hopes of being able to prevent or put an end to all armed conflicts through international arbitration are likely to continue to prove illusory. The unworldliness of any such expectations is illustrated by an appeal which the Indian politician Mahatma Gandhi addressed to Hitler while Britain was standing alone during the Second World War:

'My dear friend,

It is not a formality that I address you as "friend". I have no enemies. Your own writings and speeches, as well those of your friends and admirers, leave no doubt that many of your actions are unnatural and incompatible with human dignity. Particularly people like myself, who believe in the universal brotherhood of man, think like this... For this reason we cannot hope that you will win the war...By having success in war you have not proved that you are right. You prove only that your power to destroy is greater...I find it hard to believe that you do not understand that this capacity for destruction is not exclusive to anyone. If not Great Britain, then some other power will certainly make use of it and beat you with your own weapons...I therefore beg you, in the name of humanity: "Stop the war!" You will not lose anything if you place all the quarrels between yourself and Great Britain before an international tribunal, in the composition of which you would have a voice.'

This incredible example of political naïvety is by no means unique. In attempts to deceive and reassure itself, there appear to be no lengths to which the human mind will not go. The Swedish chemist Alfred Nobel was a lifelong pacifist who regarded his invention of dynamite in 1867 as a means of ensuring national defence. He expected the possession of dynamite to deter attack and so to introduce an era of lasting worldwide peace. Clever as he was, Nobel remained unable to perceive how fundamental human nature must guarantee an eager welcome for any new explosives as an enhancement of *offensive* capacity. In a spirit similar to that of Nobel, the Pole Ivan Bloch produced a book in 1897 in which he argued that there could be no more wars, since the increased firepower of modern weapons would make warfare too horrendous.

It is not known whether Bloch was still alive in 1914, and if so, how he then reacted to the events unfolding. A full hundred years after Bloch's monstrous piece of self-deception we should at least make an effort to apply a rather better developed sense of realism to the problems of preserving peace and freedom. Yes, freedom too is part of this complex of war and peace; it is even to a large extent the core, since we more developed peoples are basically prepared to engage in warfare only in order to defend or restore our own freedom or those of others.

In this effort of self-sacrifice for the sake of freedom, it might well be felt that the humblest private, British or Indian, who served in the war to keep Japan out of India is infinitely more deserving of our respect and thanks than Mahatma Gandhi.

Napoleon once claimed that all his battles had been 'diplomatic steps towards peace'. It was this vision of war as diplomacy's instrument of compulsion which Clausewitz took as the foundation of his philosophy. His rationalized concept began at once to dominate the thinking of Europe's military men.

With the emergence of the 'never again' campaigns which followed the First World War, the attraction of the Clausewitz maxim started to fade. In the course of forty years of 'cold war', the notion was gradually abandoned altogether – among industrial peoples. Nonetheless, the Clausewitz way of thinking is far from dead. We shall continue to encounter less advanced countries which attempt, in the words of the great Prussian, *'to use physical force to compel the other fellow to do what we want'*. We shall continue to have to deal with states and peoples who try to spread their ideology or their religion with the sword. In other words: Clausewitz is dead, but has not died. Or has died but is not dead.

Numerous theories have been evolved and argued in an effort to explain the origins of war. Some see war as a sort of natural catastrophe which befalls mankind at intervals. Any such negatively passive starting point will not bring us very much further. Others have detected in the wars of mankind an inescapable escalation, which they believe will culminate in a great 'final war' leading us at last into an epoch of permanent peace. This is another viewpoint which does not help us very much, though it is a beguiling thought that one great nuclear war might after all prove to be enough, driving mankind finally to its senses. Further hypotheses presume to find the origins of wars in armaments themselves. According to the subscribers to this theory, an arms race itself must sooner or later erupt into war when disagreements arise. Along with Clausewitz, this argument too became a casualty of the 'Cold War', when the greatest level of deployed arms in history failed to lead to war.

The British researcher Lewis Richardson tackled the question rather more scientifically after the First World War, undertaking the complex task of analysing international relations before that conflict from as many perspectives as possible. Starting with 1908, when the European arms build-up had begun, Richardson broke down all the data on which he could lay his hands. When he had finished, he concluded that arms procurement and foreign trade were the deciding factors in international affairs, and devised mathematical formulae to relate these two determinants to one another. The pictures produced by these formulae should, Richardson hoped, make it possible to recognize when a danger point was being reached. According to his own calculations, if the differential between the total defence spending of the powers involved and the volume of their joint trade had been a mere £5,000,000 lower, the First World War would never have broken out.

And, of course, there are fairies at the bottom of my garden.

As praiseworthy and unquestionably well meaning as are all such attempts to detect, and warn of, dangerous courses, researches of this kind are doomed to failure from the start, because they are concerned solely with *measurable* factors. The explosive value of a chemical element can be expressed in figures, and so can the pressure inside a boiler – but the degree of underlying harmony or dissatisfaction in human relations can not. There is neither sense nor purpose in devising hypotheses of this kind without including in our considerations the motivating emotions of the peoples concerned or variables such as their governments' sober-mindedness, resolution,

227

strength of nerve or readiness to take risks. With or without a difference of £5,000,000 in the pre-1914 gap between foreign trade and arms spending, the French would still have been driven by their urge for revenge on the Prussians, Germans would have remained just as boastful, continuing to put up other people's backs, and Russia's actions would all the same have been impelled by her sense of mission to lead the Slav peoples in a crusade against domination by the Germanic nations.

Scientists admit that they know of no more complicated structure in the universe than the human brain. No wonder, then, that human behaviour is likely to remain an object of never-ending research. Investigations into the problem areas of peace and war are a waste of time if they proceed from any starting points other than considerations of the human psyche. Lewis Richardson did not ignore psychological factors; he was fully aware of them. His well-intentioned Quaker sincerity foundered on the impossibility of quantifying these.

Comfortable formulae of the kind beloved of both charlatans and serious researchers become meaningless when faced with the extreme complexity and range of human relations and the influence upon them of both reasoning and emotions. We can never quantify deterrence, nor can we know precisely the extent of another's aims. What is a deterrent to one may be regarded by another as a challenge. Our personal estimate of the only gains worth sacrifice and hazard could well exceed by a factor of many times the more modest aspirations found by others to be worthy of suicidal risk-taking. We can assign no accurate mathematical values to the variables of mental and emotional imbalance, lack of perspective or the want of any sense of proportion. 'Blinding with science' fulfils no purpose other than satisfying the mass need for self-delusory reassurance. Peace and war studies will never be an exact science. At the most, we can hope only to determine some rules of thumb.

Run-of-the-mill wars seem to break out because feelings have been overstrained in one way or another. At some point, one side or the other, if not both, has had enough. Disregarding and even trampling on the other fellow's sensibilities is thus the basic sin in international affairs. Naturally this does not apply to calculating wars of aggression, any more than to wars of ideology or religion. There is usually little point in treating with consideration the feelings of a nation set on spreading its beliefs, or extending its power and possessions, by force.

Pain is the inseparable companion to life. There is no existence without suffering in some form. We experience pain ourselves and inflict it on others, even if only unwillingly and accidentally. Pain is unavoidable for every living creature, and we can never eliminate it entirely from our own lives or the lives of others.

One thing we can do, and it is the most natural of all commandments: we should and must try to limit the scope of suffering to as small an extent as possible. Everyone is of course concerned to limit his own suffering. What matters is constraining the *accumulation* of pain suffered by humanity *in toto*. For each of us personally, this means that our actions must be governed by consideration of all the persons likely to be affected by them.

Governments and the United Nations must act no differently. Other peoples and states are to be treated as we in our personal lives should also treat the individuals around us. This can probably never be better expressed than in the simple formulation: Do unto others as you would have them do unto you.

National feelings need to be respected. Consciousness of belonging to one particular people is anchored deeply in human nature; it is a feeling going back to the smallest group of people in the earliest times. Xenophobia, that dislike of foreigners which all too easily can turn into hatred, originated in the fear felt by our most distant ancestors when faced by predatory rivals who were strangers to them.

If the twentieth century has any obvious lesson for us, then it is certainly this, that national feelings are stronger than any ideology. Underestimating national feelings or disregarding national self-esteem can cause a great deal of unnecessary suffering. The trend at the end of the twentieth century is unmistakably towards self-determination of all peoples. Supranational governments are already an anachronism. The seed of much potential harm is to be found in efforts to maintain supranational structures or to force them on people, whether these be arbitrarily assembled colonial territories, states contrived artificially as part of peace treaties, or attempts to force together old-established neighbouring national states into one unified agglomeration. While intermittent national arrogance undoubtedly causes many wars, the contented sovereign national state unquestionably remains the surest guarantee of harmonious living.

Preventing all wars is likely to remain an unrealizable dream. Nonetheless, we can and should strive to keep their number as small as possible. Not too much in the way of preventive action can be expected. It is always the villain who sets the pace, while the peace-loving nations are left merely to react to his moves. Any efforts to keep the peace always stumble along behind the course of events. People usually spring into action only once they have been gripped by fear, and then it is generally too late.

Only in the rarest cases are preventive measures undertaken when dangers are no more than seen to be unfolding. The emergence of a fanatical government in an unstable part of the world will be noted with concern – but this concern is rarely sufficient to register in the human brain that trouble is on the way and that timely steps of some sort are required to prevent its developing into full-scale catastrophe. The preferred way is to suppress all such thoughts, hoping that the problem will go away of its own accord. So long as it is only the brain which is telling one to act, wishful thinking and excuses will prevail. To bring about activity, the emotions must first be activated. Once the situation has become so bad that its potentially fatal consequences can no longer be overlooked, fear sets in. This fear does what the brain was unable to do: it stimulates action. Meanwhile, disaster has usually arrived right on the doorstep.

Though most people never seem to grow any wiser even from the experiences of their own lifetimes, the sum of human knowledge is there for all of us. We should learn from it. In his *Politics*, Aristotle quotes an example of common sense in antiquity which ought to make us, with our over-evaluation of ourselves as advanced humanity, blush with shame at our own obtuseness. Aristotle records how, around 350BC, the ruler of a besieged city asked the commander of the besieging army to reflect on how long it would take him to capture the place and how much would be the cost of victory even if he were successful. The defending ruler then offered to hand over the city on payment of less than that sum. The besieging commander was made to think again, and abandoned the siege. Apparently, even the price of buying the city was too high for him, and the defenders' clever offer forced him to realize that warfare, exacting an even higher cost, was simply not worth it.

One of the things which history teaches is that the early years of a new state resemble the childhood and adolescence of the individual. Years of ignorance and awkwardness are followed by a flexing of muscles, after which the one will become responsible and mature, the other unpredictable and dangerous, according to circumstances, experience and the degree of innate common sense available in the individual or the nation.

The expression 'family of nations' is frequently heard, and it is indeed helpful to bear such a metaphor in mind. Like any individual human family, the world family of peoples comprises many diverse members with varying abilities and characters. The difference is that in the family of nations there is no firm order. In no sensibly run family would the keys to a 200mph Jaguar be handed to a ten-year-old, nor would the father let a six-year-old play with his shotgun. In crass contrast, every member state at the United Nations General Assembly enjoys the same voting rights – just as if children were allowed a voice in life-threatening family matters.

Precipitate dissolution of colonial rule has launched onto the world scene sovereign states armed with modern weapons and with rulers whose level of competence is well demonstrated by the drastic decline in their countries' prosperity and levels of personal freedom since their European governors left the scene. It is the innocent and helpless people in these countries who are the ones to suffer, the ones to endure the greatest material hardship, the ones to die in unnecessary massacres and wars.

If we really care about our fellow-humans, if we are genuinely concerned to prevent or to limit the extent of their suffering, we cannot be content to watch the proliferation of ever-worsening dictatorships and bloodshed. It is a poor excuse for inaction to remind ourselves that colonial rule is felt to have 'exploited' subject peoples. This is not necessarily how the tortured people of Angola remember the Portuguese. Somewhere between colonial rule by outsiders and the independence which has saddled many former subject peoples with bloody dictatorship by their fellows, it ought to be possible to find a middle way to ensure prosperity and physical security for the mass of ordinary humanity in these territories. It cannot be beyond man's ingenuity to devise means whereby the most capable nations can help to administer poor countries for the benefit of indigenous peoples, not for their own gain.

There should certainly be no hesitation about stepping in to prevent Third World countries from coming into possession of atomic or other weapons of mass destruction, even accepting that such a supervisory role is likely in the long run to bring about just that very resentment which one should be at pains to prevent. In the case of India and Pakistan, the opportunity to do this has already been missed – an act of neglect which there is still time, but probably no willpower, to put right.

Any such intervention is of course fraught with difficulties. It also requires just the sort of decisiveness of action which, to judge by the UN's performance to date, would be asking simply too much. Who is to decide whether, and in what country or countries, checks are to be made? Who will carry these out? If entry to a country or to a plant is refused, what means may be used to perform an inspection? Should the construction of nuclear weapons be forbidden also to nations which can produce convincing arguments that these are necessary for self-defence, principally for deterrence?

Israel, for example, is demonstrably surrounded by mortal enemies, some of whom deny her right to exist. Should the great powers force their way into Israel, to confiscate any nuclear weapons and to dismantle any facilities for building them? Would it be right to forbid possession of nuclear weapons to a state in such a

232

precarious position as Israel, as a result perhaps delivering her into the hands of her enemies?

What about generally valid international law with its concepts of sovereignty and the sacrosanct nature of domestic affairs, and what about the exigencies of national defence? Is international law to be set aside in the interests of international security, simply on suspicion? Who would decide, who would carry out the measures deemed necessary? The problems are manifold, but it is precisely for dealing with these that we elect our parliamentarians and pay our taxes. To expect something to be done is not asking too much.

On the other hand, perhaps it is. While former colonies have been becoming progressively more repressive and warlike, the quality of parliamentarians in our western democracies has declined visibly, in terms of both intellect and character. What is worse, these deteriorating standards have scarcely attracted attention, let alone protest. We have witnessed the passive acceptance even of presidential lying under oath – a crime striking at the very structure of the rule of law which is supposedly the foundation of a civilized society. A nation which tolerates this sort of thing in its leaders is likely to have little to offer when the test of its moral fibre has to be faced. It may be true that, as the French diplomat Joseph de Maistre observed, each country has the government which it deserves. The trouble is that the foolish drag the sensible down with them.

Both Aristotle and Plato (the latter apparently also quoting Socrates, as well as speaking for himself) warned that democracies evolve inevitably into tyrannies. Though such a suggestion may seem at first sight startling, the reasoning behind this fear is that an excess of individual freedom fragments national will, producing the necessity of, and demand for, no-nonsense government with an unequivocal direction in policy. It is indeed arguable that Hitler came to power at least partly because of the lack of any clear course in the Weimar Republic, with its chaotic moral licence and proliferation of political ideas. More than forty divergent parties fought for the electorate's favour, resulting in no fewer than fifteen different elected democratic governments in only fourteen years. Fragmentation within society, just as in Parliament, can prove as fatal to us as it was to the Weimar Republic. An unshakeable level of national unity is the essential foundation for survival in war. The dismal overall performances of Italians in World War Two and Americans in Vietnam were symptomatic of the divided societies from which their troops were drawn. In neither case was the nation's heart firmly in the struggle.

The much-vaunted 'multicultural society', of which so many self-deceivers appear inexplicably to be proud, can rebound with lethal effects, leaving future generations to shake their heads in disbelief that we could have been so short-sighted. Publicly, at least, no one appears yet to have asked himself what might be the consequences of our being forced into war against, say, an Islamic state having a million or more adherents resident in the UK. In a modern industrial state, possibilities for sabotage are ubiquitous; within a composite population, opportunities for civil war manifold.

Only adherence to a common set of values can assure harmony in, and survival of, any society. It is an inexorable law that armed forces reflect the social order from which they are drawn. If there is no unified purpose at home, there can be none in the field.

Rome collapsed after admitting all the scum of her empire as citizens. We have no need to commit this same error, being more than capable of producing a superfluity of native scum of our own, without importing additional numbers into our grotesquely overcrowded islands. The creators and proponents of 'multi-cultural' populations are mightily pleased with themselves. Future generations are likely to curse them. In defence matters, wilful blindness can be national suicide. Societies less tolerant than our own, taking a more realistic view of humanity, will not fall into the same errors of misjudgement.

For safety's sake it must be assumed on principle that even the most sophisticated surveillance systems (satellite cameras and the like) can be deceived and put out of action, and that the secret assembly of nuclear warheads can be disguised by means other than the construction of atomic power stations. In the age of nuclear weapons and guided missiles there remains one paramount rule: Trust no one, not even the smallest.

On the positive side, modern arms now give us the opportunity to do something denied to earlier generations: they provide the means of ending the nonsensical round of tit for tat exchanges of violence which has determined the course of human history to date and which still defines life in certain parts of the globe.

It is wasted effort to inflict merely physical defeat which leaves the vanquished aggressor feeling that he can do better next time. The nature of the rout which he suffers must be such that it is not just the aggressor's armed power but his national psyche which is overthrown.

It is clear that nothing less than a transformation in mental attitude can bring about genuinely heartfelt abandonment of war as a means of pursuing political ends. Fundamental change of this kind can be effected only by undergoing shock of such magnitude – the Carnoustie effect raised to the power of n – that a trauma is inflicted whose effects linger in the collective consciousness of a people for generations thereafter.

This means no more pussyfooting around a problem, no more repetitive 'peace' conferences and meaningless 'cease-fires'. Such devastation has to be inflicted on an erring nation that survivors curse the leaders who brought them to it, while their successors continue in mortal fear of any more military adventures.

Retaliation is the self-perpetuating boomerang of the limited intellect. Where there is no capacity for clear vision, massive psychological trauma can at least induce life-saving inhibition.

Nothing in human experience to date suggests than anything works as well in keeping the peace as instilling fear. Deterrence through overwhelming and irresistible destructive power is not merely an option; it is our only promising course.

If we fail in this, through shortsightedness, misconception, erroneous goodwill or sheer stupidity, it will be, as always, the innocent and simple people of this earth, including those of our own flesh and blood, who will suffer for our folly.

How much we really care about our own future generations will be demonstrated – and their destiny will be determined – not by our humanitarian notions and intentions, but by what we do.

THE SEVEN DEADLY SINS AND THE TEN COMMANDMENTS OF WAR

Exact study of events shows that most disasters are caused by errors in planning, not in execution.

Summarizing, the following deadly sins can be identified:

rushing too quickly into war;

leaving it too late before going to war;

continuing to fight on in war when the objective can no longer be attained;

breaking off hostilities too soon (leaving the objective unattained);

extending the scope of a war unnecessarily;

neglecting or losing the support (including moral support) of third party countries;

tying one's hands in advance through treaties of alliance.

The paradoxes here are all too apparent, suggesting that whatever one does, it will turn out to be wrong and possibly self-defeating.

This only confirms how high a degree of insight and judgement is demanded in foreign policy. A statesman must demonstrate the ability to think himself into the other fellow's situation, his feelings and his way of thinking; he must be able to understand these and to act towards him accordingly. How many politicians can be trusted to bring these qualities to the task? In view of the far greater destructive potential of future wars, the standard of personal abilities demanded of statesmen is higher than ever before, yet everyday affairs show all too clearly that the intellectual qualities and integrity of character of most politicians lie significantly below the level required of them by the responsibility attached to their positions.

Their task is admittedly not an easy one. Critics always have the easier job. Developing the necessary fine level of judgement demands much more than is required simply to list the seven deadly sins of war – or even the ten commandments:

Undertake everything possible diplomatically to prevent matters developing into war, without conceding to a potential aggressor anything which might encourage him in his actions;

remain strong enough to try to deter possible aggressors, but do not upset their feelings and never do anything which can act as a challenge to them. Issue no premature or inflexible ultimatums;

ensure that you always have the best armaments available and are capable of fighting any kind of war which an enemy might force on you, in order to end any hostilities as quickly as possible and so with minimum losses;

do not rely on superior technology alone, but ensure that the nation is morally prepared for the demands of war and equal to these;

do not allow yourself to be blinded by your own strengths and capabilities, but always remember those superior forces and nations who were brought down in the past by over-confidence;

do not count on the reliability of allies, either before or during a war, and remember that they may have quite different objectives from your own. Mistake this, and you could find that you have fought a war for nothing;

never lose forward momentum in war – including the moral dynamics;

never forget that your aim in war must be to reduce to a minimum the amount of human suffering. Always be prepared therefore to conclude a compromise peace, and leave the enemy a way out which will enable him to agree to a cease-fire without humiliation. Never demand his unconditional capitulation;

do not conclude peace at any price or a peace which will render pointless the sacrifices of your soldiers;

give your defeated enemy no reason or excuse to reopen hostilities, but conclude a just peace. Treat the defeated opponent as you would wish to be treated yourself in his place.

Unless driven solely by vanity or the hunger for power, most people who enter politics are motivated to some extent by the vision of an ideal or at least of a greatly improved society. Social questions of work, incomes, education, health, housing or transport, of trade, economy, industry or the environment are what constitute the world of their thoughts and concerns.

He would be a *rara avis* indeed who became a candidate for parliament primarily out of concern for the military protection of his country. Yet the defence of its citizens remains, as it was when organized society first evolved, the primary function of the state.

Though many believe that they know a lot about it because they once read a one-sided book on the Second World War, most politicians have absolutely no idea of the causes of war or of warfare itself. Yet ignorance and lack of ability in just these fields are immeasurably more dangerous than the same inadequacies in any other sphere.

Political engagement in social matters tends to proceed from emotional involvement. In questions of peace and war, on the other hand, feelings have to be subdued, with cool and detached reasoning the prime commandment.

Every urge to revenge, for example, must be suppressed. Emotions cannot be completely eradicated, though, and it would be foolish either to demand or to expect this. All the same, feelings have to remain subordinate; they should be man's servants, not his master.

Of course emotions have their place. The love of justice, of intellectual freedom, of truth, are feelings which we should not only tolerate but indeed encourage.

Horror at the mistreatment of our fellow humans, at the abuse of their freedoms and rights, at brutality – an upsurge of outraged sensations in such cases is natural to any civilized human being. If we do not feel repugnance, anger or revulsion in such cases, then we are ourselves no more than miserable specimens of the lower types of living creatures, and need never have bothered to enter the world in human form at all.

Reactions of distress in the face of injustice or brutality should, as it were, loose off the starting pistol, but not direct our actions; deeds are to be determined solely by rational thought.

To learn from the mistakes of the past is not just elementary; it is our prime duty.

'The saying about war as a continuation of politics has become a catchword, and is therefore dangerous. One can equally well say: War is the bankruptcy of politics.'
– Generaloberst Hans von Seeckt (1866-1936), Commander-in-Chief of the German Army, 1920-26

A LAST-MINUTE APOLOGY

Inexcusably, errors which crept in during repeated electronic transfers of text from computer to computer via differing word processing programmes were not noticed until pages 1 to 239 were ready to print.

These disfigurements range from the mysterious appearance of digits in the middle of a word to the inexplicable omission of with in a sentence on p.55 which should include the phrase 'the persistence with which'.

The author apologizes for these blemishes, which are his sole responsibility. They would have been easy to eliminate at the beginning, and proved impossible of correction later.

This experience may serve as an analagous reminder: However difficult it may be to avert a war, it is always easier than fighting one.

Gordon Lang
Carnoustie, 2002